C000059876

ELEANOR YULE is a Scottish writer, film director
She is best known for her feature film *Blinded*
for the BBC with Michael Palin. She lives in the ......
a large ginger cat.

DAVID MANDERSON is a writer and academic. His publications include novels
and collections which contributed to the Research Excellence Framework.
He lectures in fiction writing and narrative at the University of the West of
Scotland.

Open Scotland is a series which aims to open up debate about the future of
Scotland and do this by challenging the closed nature of many conversations,
assumptions and parts of society. It is based on the belief that the closed
Scotland has to be understood, and that this is a pre-requisite for the kind of
debate and change society needs to have to challenge the status quo. It does this
in a non-partisan, pluralist and open-minded manner, which contributes to
making the idea of self-government into a genuine discussion about the prospects
and possibilities of social change.

Commissioning Editor: Gerry Hassan

Luath Press is an independently owned and managed book publishing company
based in Scotland, and is not aligned to any political party or grouping.
Viewpoints is an occasional series exploring issues of current and future
relevance.

The Glass Half Full

Moving Beyond Scottish Miserabilism

ELEANOR YULE and DAVID MANDERSON

Luath Press Limited

EDINBURGH

www.luath.co.uk

First published 2014

ISBN: 978-1-910021-34-7

The paper used in this book is recyclable. It is made from
low chlorine pulps produced in a low energy, low emissions manner
from renewable forests.

Printed and bound by
Bell & Bain Ltd., Glasgow

Typeset in 11 point Sabon
by 3btype.com

The authors' right to be identified as author of this work under the
Copyright, Designs and Patents Act 1988 has been asserted.

© Eleanor Yule and David Manderson, 2014

MISERABLE

Wretched, exceedingly unhappy, causing misery, extremely poor or mean, contemptible

THE CONCISE ENGLISH DICTIONARY

MISERABLE

1 unhappy or depressed; wretched
2 causing misery, discomfort, etc: *a miserable life*
3 Contemptible: *a miserable villain*
4 Sordid or squalid: *miserable living conditions*
5 Chiefly austral. *Mean, stingy*
6 (Pejorative intensifier): *you miserable wretch.* (C16: from old French, from Latin *miserabilis*, worthy of pity, from *miserari* to pity, from miser wretched

COLLINS ENGLISH DICTIONARY

SCOTTISH MISERABLISM

A drowsy addiction to imagined injury

ANDREW O'HAGAN, London Review of Books

SCOTS MISERABLISM

Marked out by their tragic tone miserabilist screenworks depict the lives of violent and addicted anti-heroes set against the backdrop of post-industrial hopelessness, urban squalor and decay. Where redemption and forgiveness seem impossible without exile from Scotland, and where the hero struggles to develop tools or strategies to ultimately overcome his misery or 'temptations'.

ELEANOR YULE

Contents

Acknowledgements

This book is a joint endeavour between the two of us and a collaboration in its ideas and content. Many thanks to Gerry Hassan for commissioning this book, and to Beth Armstrong, Andrew Lyons and Jim Sullivan.

Prologue

ELEANOR YULE

TOWERING AND MAGNIFICENT, the *Queen Mary* passenger liner, like many of Scotland's world-class celebrities, resides far from home. She was decommissioned and preserved close to the shores to which she carried many of Scotland's talented sons and daughters who, like her, would never return home.

Built in the '30s by John Brown and Company, shipbuilders in Clydebank, she was both a technical and aesthetic triumph. Twice the weight of the Titanic and with faster engines by far, she is 12 decks high and boasts ten million expertly placed rivets. At any one time a community of 3,000 highly skilled men worked together on the construction of a sublime feminine form that would go on to grace the high seas.

Her 81,000 tons of steel sit eternally anchored at Long Island in a purpose built dry dock. She is now an American tourist attraction and celebrated as an Art Deco masterpiece. Her miles of beautifully preserved wood-lined corridors, mirrored, marble ballrooms and polished brass piano bars are crafted to perfection; even her Bakelite air vents are works of art. Her glamorous history continues to attract crowds of enthusiastic visitors. And, like any good Scottish creation, there's a dark side. An aimless phantom haunts the ladies changing rooms in the cavernous bowels of her titanic hull; its digitally simulated appearance is a big hit with the tourists.

On the ship's completion in 1936 she was heralded as a symbol of world-class Scottish engineering and design and an icon of the Empire. Her launch was celebrated as a sign of British industry returning to work after the Great Depression, which had halted the completion of the ship and marked the first cracks in the eventual shattering of the UK's heavy industries, and the economic division of the country between the wealthy South and the grim North.

The long post-war decline of the shipyards, mines and steelworks hit the highly skilled labouring class in Scotland. The mass unemployment of the '80s forced these proud workers into unsatisfying unskilled jobs, or into the long humiliating queues that wound around the 'buroo'. In this new landscape the skilled riveter, responsible for ensuring a ship was watertight, was worthless and his craftsmanship non-transferable. The modernist dream of purpose-built council schemes to house this 'problematic class' quickly became a no-man's-land, a bleak post-industrial waste ground for impoverished hard men and anxious, overworked women.

New survival skills would emerge among the unemployed male working classes, particularly in the north, where climate contributed to the atmosphere of depression. Violence, addiction and black humour would help men survive the new landscape of poverty and worthlessness, not to mention the boredom of their rudderless existence.

In Scotland a new sensibility began to emerge as things declined, a close cousin of naturalist literature and British social realism. 'Clydesidism' oozed out of the pens of Scottish writers like William McIlvanney, James Kelman and screenwriter Peter McDougall, exposing the plight of these proud forgotten men. 'Clydesidism' was identified by film theorist Duncan Petrie as an important reaction to the other extreme, the over-idealised depictions of a rural Scotland, the quaint, the twee, the world of *Brigadoon* and *Para Handy*, a land of tartan, shortbread and the Kailyard.

By the '80s and the peak of Margaret Thatcher's reign, 'Miserablism' had seized Scotland's fictional imagination and at its centre, the 'Miserablist' hero loomed large. Born as a fearless protester, fighting for his dignity, four decades later he has become a macho stereotype, a cultural victim, stuck in a cycle of hopelessness, an urban Scotsman with little to be proud of and a chip on his shoulder the size of the *Queen Mary*.

There's a much quoted and telling sequence in *Trainspotting* (1996), the film adaptation of Irvine Welsh's bestselling novel. In it, the athletic and clean cut Tommy (Kevin McKidd), takes his heroin-addicted mates on a train ride hoping to tempt them away from their self-destructive lifestyles by showing them the great outdoors and instilling in them a sense of pride in their own country. The miserablist hero, Renton (Ewan McGregor), takes one look at the breathtaking view of the hills and tells the beleaguered Tommy exactly what he thinks:

> It's shite being Scottish, we are the lowest of the low, the scum of the fucking earth, the most wretched, miserable, servile, pathetic trash

that was ever shat into civilisation. Some people hate the English, I don't, they're just wankers. We on the other hand are colonised by wankers, can't even find a decent culture to be colonised by. We are ruled by effete arseholes. It's a shite state of affairs... and all the fresh air in the world won't make any fucking difference.

This starts Tommy, one of the most tragic characters in the miserablist canon, on a downward spiral from a positive, healthy character in a loving relationship to a heroin-addicted recluse with AIDS, who is later found dead, his eyes eaten out by worms.

So if *Trainspotting* and miserablism in general give us a glimpse into the Scottish psyche, what does this tell us about ourselves? Have we turned our backs on our heritage, our landscape and our diversity and redefined ourselves as not just rivals with the English but inferior to them? When did we become cultural victims? And the bigger question is: how useful is it for us to keep replaying the same stuck record? Is it time to move away from an image of Scotland that constantly casts it as the poor relation? Do we have a responsibility to project other images of Scotland and Scottishness that show our culture's richness and diversity? And how will we do that if most of the editorial and financial decisions are still being made in the capital of a country that we believe are our oppressors?

Introduction

ELEANOR YULE

Oh, the British politicians, they haven't made a hit,
They are ruining the country more than just a bit,
If they keep on the way that they're goin' we'll all be in the jobbie,
So you better get your feet in your wellies.

BILLY CONNOLLY – *The Great Northern Welly-Boot Show*

IRONICALLY IT WAS the threat of shipyard closure in Scotland and the lack of work for Scottish actors that meant I would grow up a stranger to my own land.

Although born and bred in Glasgow, I spent my childhood far south of the border. My parents were part of a steady hemorrhage of skill and talent from Scotland which meant, at its peak, 50,000 people, one percent of the population, left Scotland in one year for more promising lands.

My parents, both Scottish actors, were performing alongside Billy Connolly in *The Great Northern Welly-Boot Show* when they jumped ship. The show had taken the Edinburgh Fringe by storm in 1972 and shortly afterwards transferred to London. My parents, like some others in the Scottish cast and crew, decided to stay on in England indefinitely and join the legions of expatriate Scots scattered around the leafy suburbs of what is now the M25. For a Scottish actor, the streets of London were paved with gold. With its packed audition rooms and well-connected agents, England was a land of opportunity compared to the modestly paid repertory theatre and occasional TV roles on offer back in Scotland. Despite the jump, my mother, actress Katherine Stark, never did manage to throw off the mantle of playing prostitutes or addicted mothers. She went down to England playing a Glaswegian tart and, as an actress with a Scottish accent, it stayed that way for most of her career. Much of this typecasting was down to a lack of female roles for Scottish actresses and the dominance of miserablism. My mother would reappear in an iconic role in one of the most significant works of the miserablist movement, Peter McDougall's *Just a Boy's Game*. My father, John Yule, on the other hand, fared rather better. A steady stream of Censored aftershave adverts, a few Hammer Horror films and a variety of parts in Scottish Kailyard drama series for the UK networks kept the wolf from our door.

The Welly-Boot Show launched many Scots careers. Actor Bill Paterson, director Robin Lefevre and Billy Connolly have all found success through it, and fared far better than the doomed shipyard workers the comic satire was about. The play introduced the London luvvies to the grim struggles of the north, and the plight of the Upper Clyde Shipyard workers who were fighting Edward Heath's government to keep their jobs. Their cause was championed by gifted orator Jimmy Reid, who was satirised in the show and played by Connolly. Reid did save the shipyards and the livelihood of his men, and although at the time the outcome was hopeful, Thatcher's succession meant the war was far from over. The dignity of the worker was already tragically compromised.

It was not until Glasgow was named European City of Culture in 1990 that I was able to return to my home city. Transformed, and undergoing a cultural manicure, it was almost unrecognisable from the depressed and darkly pessimistic city my parents had left in the '70s. The Garden Festival site had started to transfigure the Clyde into a decorative asset, with the Finnieston Crane a lonely vestige of its industrial past. Glasgow as City of Culture followed shortly afterwards and set about reconstructing the depressed communities of the schemes into 'actors' and participants in colourful street theatre, while the explosion of Mackintosh mania and the presence of Nina Simone, Robert Lepage and Peter Brook in the Southside's Tramway Theatre brought visitors from all over the world to a newly colourful, cosmopolitan Glasgow.

As a trainee at BBC Scotland, I was one of an intake of nine bright young things chosen by the BBC bosses to help ensure BBC Scotland's broadcasting future. Even so, the award-winning BBC Scotland film unit was being dismantled as I arrived. Under Pharic Maclaren's visionary leadership there had been a golden age of Scottish television, eclectic and representative of the nation's talent. The film unit produced countless adaptations of Scottish classics such as Stevenson's unfinished masterpiece The Weir of Hermiston and Grassic Gibbon's Sunset Song. Historical Scottish dramas like The Eagle of the Ninth (recently remade as a feature film) and Boswell, starring a young Brian Cox, were all being produced for the BBC network. In contrast were the Kailyard stalwarts such as the long running and popular *Para Handy* and the legal drama series *Sutherland's Law*. New writing was also represented in plays such as John Byrne's debut *The Slab Boys* (1979), while cutting edge social realism for the Wednesday Play strand all emerged from the same unit. The whole of Scotland was represented on television, across all classes, not just the Central Belt and not just Glasgow.

'Producers choice' changed things. This term, like almost all BBC generated jargon, was a euphemism for cost-cutting. Under John Birt, Director General of the BBC between 1992 and 2000, Auntie's doors would be thrown open to competition from the freelance world. The Reithian ethos to educate, inform and entertain would now include a pressure on producers to cut costs and pursue ratings, celebrity-driven content and format shows. This Thatcherite ethos also created a growing suspicion of 'artists', 'writers' and 'new talent'. The emphasis was firmly on production and productivity, with a nod, of course, to quality, and a newly created generation of thrusting 'Assistant Producers', 'Heads of Department' and 'Programme Controllers' would march Auntie through her seismic change.

Increasingly, 'savings' across programming meant a reduction in filming budgets, making locations restricted. It was cheaper to film in the Central Belt, particularly in drama where transporting cast and crew to the Highlands and Islands, for example, soon became a luxury. Editorial power also began to shift towards London. In one surreal commissioning meeting we realised that the 'Strand Controller' of the arts, a Hampstead resident, had never heard of Charles Rennie Mackintosh. On that occasion we got the benefit of the doubt and a film was commissioned, but there were many other occasions where great Scottish subjects and writers were overlooked due to a London commissioner's lack of knowledge about the Scottish cultural landscape. But what the commissioners did know about Scotland was miserablism. This particular representation of Scottishness had an impressive track record, had showcased some of the best Scottish writing and acting talent, and was a safe bet.

I was one of the new kids on the block and, not surprisingly, distrusted by the BBC old guard, the long term members of staff who were highly unionised (not unlike the workers on the Clyde) and from a generation of men not used to female bosses.

One of the first shoots I directed for the BBC taught me to navigate the male-dominated industry in Scotland with caution. I'd broken etiquette and spoken directly to the 'spark' or electrician who was fixing the lights rather than going through his boss, the 'lighting cameraman'. Furious at my lack of decorum the spark threw a chair at me. At film school we had just worked together in teams. At the BBC, even in the '90s, it was another ball game, and one where women were best seen typing in an office and not in charge on the film set. Nevertheless our numbers were swelling and we moved through the ranks, particularly on the production side. Women were a good fit in production as hard working, backstage organisers, but were much less visible in the front-line creative jobs.

When I was expecting my first child at the age of 25 I looked around and saw that as a pregnant, female, TV director there was no one else like me. I was so alarmed by my apparent isolation I hid my bump for five months before revealing it to my boss who saw it as a large inconvenience. A well-known presenter saw my swollen belly in the lift one day and thought it was a joke – she told me I could remove the cushion, and was horrified when I told her it was real.

It was not until the end of the '90s, however, when I left my staff job at the BBC to venture into the world of film, that I began to hear the term 'miserable' used to describe many of the film ideas that were being submitted to Scottish Screen for development. I'd had an attempt myself, with various film projects and strong producers, to buck the gritty realist trend, with projects such as *The Glasgow Girls* with *Bondagers* writer Sue Glover about a group of female artists; *The Lantern Bearers* by Bearsden novelist Ronald Frame, set in '50s Kirkcudbright with themes of music and adolescent homosexual love; and *Easy* with award winning writer Nicola McCartney and 7:84 producer John McGrath about date rape.

There were many reasons why the projects failed. Much of the problem was my lack of 'bankability' as a first-time director, but the standout films that were produced around that time, such as Lynne Ramsay's *Ratcatcher* (1996), Gillies MacKinnon's *Small Faces* (1996) and Peter Mullan's *Orphans* (1998), although skilfully made by talented directors, all bore the stamp of 'Miserablist Cinema'. Interestingly neither MacKinnon nor Ramsay had been known for their miserablist sensibilities prior to being funded in Scotland. MacKinnon's breakthrough film *The Grass Arena* (1992), a tramp to fame story, was praised for its uplifting sense of redemption, yet on his return to Scotland he chose to revisit the late '60s razor gangs, sexism and violence of his youth in his fiction. In the same vein, Ramsay's short films, made while at the National Film School in Beaconsfield, *Kill the Day* (1996) and *Small Deaths* (1996), were episodic lyrical pieces with a sense of poetic realism and female protagonists. For her first full-length feature, funded substantially by the Scottish purse, she choose a male protagonist and the depressed Scottish landscape of the '70s, the historical heartland of the miserabilist screenwriter, an era which Peter Mullan recently revisited in his feature film *Neds* (2010).

So although miserablism may have its roots in the past and have emerged out of the demise of Scotland's heavy industries and the subsequent economic depression, as an aesthetic it dominated our screens, its grip tightening around the Scottish imagination long after its inception.

On the day of the 2011 Scottish BAFTA awards journalist Teddy Jamieson wrote an article for *The Herald* highlighting the dominance of miserablism across all categories of nomination:

> Peter Mullan's film *Neds*, with its vision of 1970s gangland culture in Glasgow; the voyeuristic documentary *The Scheme*, which followed drink and drug-blurred lives on a Kilmarnock council estate; [and] even the return of Govan's favourite string-vested 'scum', *Rab C Nesbitt*. What is their Scotland? It's an urban Scotland, it's usually a Glaswegian Scotland and it's a grey, dreary, defeated, often dangerous Scotland. Yes, there's still humour there but it's a humour riddled with despair. It's a vision of a country that is alcoholic rather than merry, that is ground down rather than fighting back. It's as if someone had turned out the lights and plunged all of us viewers into the dark.

It was on an artists' retreat in the Borders in 2009 that I began to think about this subject and its relationship to my career which up until then, although relatively successful, had also been frustrating, particularly when it came to film development and trying to raise money for female driven narratives.

This led me to think that the health of a nation is reflected in its creative imagination and the way in which it chooses to project itself, and that within Scottish cinema a dark strand had emerged that chose to project a narrow and negative view of the nation. Around this time I was asked to give a talk about the way poverty had and was being depicted within Scottish film, hoping it might shed some light into the Scottish creative psyche and its dark tendencies. My response was immediate. 'Do you mean miserablism?' I asked. I then decided to concentrate on Scottish cinema output and original screenplays. There is so much to be said solely about miserablism in the Scottish televisual context, but I chose to narrow my focus to films for the purposes of the talk.

My aim for the talk was that it would be an uncompromising insider's point of view, not an academic presentation or an attempt to be conclusive, but a springboard – a starting point for discussion. I would try to bring this aesthetic or whatever it was out into the open and look at its evolution, acknowledge its merits and tackle its dominance, and by consequence its suppression of diversity, and of Scotland's many other unrepresented voices. It would not be a call for censorship. It was important to show that miserablism also had a truthful tale to tell and one that needed to be heard. But it was a voice that had become loud and overbearing, drowning out other truths about what it is to be Scottish that also need to be told.

And so I began a journey of discovery. What followed, which is described in this book, is only the tip of the iceberg, and it is ground that many academics, pundits and journalists have trodden before, but one question that still needs to be answered fully is why is miserablism so enduring? One good reason may be that historically one of Scotland's truths is its history of poverty and inequality. However, economically that has been changing. Scottish poverty fell significantly under Tony Blair between 1997 and 2007 during the peak of miserablist film production, and relatively speaking Scotland is a developed, wealthy nation, despite some deprivation and inequality. UK government figures show that Scotland is the richest part of the UK per head outside of London and the South East, and that's without the oil. Yet the Scottish perception of itself, certainly within miserablism, is as a poor, small and frustrated nation. So if miserablism is not reflecting a current truth – what is it reflecting?

First, I set out to define miserablism. What exactly is it? How does it differ from British Social Realism? Does it have genre distinctions? Having been trained in screenwriting guru Philip Parker's methodology for analysing genre his model seemed an appropriate starting point. This involved a content analysis of key miserablist screenworks looking for patterns between the theme (the emotion which drives the film), the genre (most miserablist films are personal dramas and on rare occasions thrillers) and the tone – which within the miserablist canon tends, not surprisingly, to be tragic.

The films I chose as key miserablist texts also showcase some of the best Scottish talent across all areas of production and, certainly on an aesthetic level, they give us much to be proud of as a nation. However it seems that in the area of storytelling and characterisation, the miserablist auteur always spins the same sad and sorry tale. Films I have included in my analysis are *The Brothers* (1947), Bill Douglas's *Childhood Trilogy* (1972–8), Peter McDougall's television screenplays (1972–93), the adaptation of William McIlvanney's *The Big Man* (1990), Paul Ferris's *The Wee Man* (2012), Peter Mullan's short films *Close* (1993) and *Fridge* (1995) and recent feature film *Neds* (2010), Lynne Ramsay's *Ratcatcher* (1999), David Mackenzie's *Young Adam* (2003), Gillies MacKinnon's *Small Faces* (1996), Morag McKinnon's *Donkeys* (2010), Danny Boyle's *Trainspotting* (1996), Ken Loach's *Sweet Sixteen* (2002) and Raindog's *Wasted* (2009).

Looking at the character arc, meaning the protagonist's progress across the narrative, was important. What type of characters dominated the narratives and did they have similar trajectories? Setting, atmosphere, lighting and production values all came into to it, and also the economic and editorial decisions that were being made to commission these works. Where, in fact, was the hunger to commission this content coming from? Who was making the editorial decisions? What kind of audiences were they trying to attract?

The result of all this would be a hybrid argument, a polemic closer to a self-help book than an academic treatise. There has never been any intention that it should be definitive, but rather just a starting point to debate miserablism's merits, and its many shortcomings.

I delivered my first lecture on a cold dark day in February in the hallowed halls of the Royal College of Physicians and Surgeons in Glasgow to a mixed audience and very few media types. Their number ranged across people working in the front lines of healthcare, politics and social work. The previous speaker in the seminar series had been Michael Meaney, a professor and a world leading expert specialising in biological psychiatry, neurology, and neurosurgery, primarily known for his research on stress, maternal care, and gene expression, so I was not sure how 'miserablism' would go down.

I hadn't imagined the subject would take the audience so much by surprise. No one had noticed, it seemed, the way in which themes of depression, subjection and violence had infiltrated our imaginations by stealth and permeated every area of culture. Reactions ranged from disappointment to shame to shock, with some members of the audience in tears as they realised the bleakness of our own vision of ourselves. Many invitations followed to repeat the talk, again to very diverse audiences across Scotland.

I have recently started to collaborate with my PhD supervisor Dr David Manderson to expand the definition more specifically into literature, as I have found that many of the key miserablist screenworks have roots in Scottish literature or were literary adaptations in the first place. We hope this new work can emphasise the more positive aspects of the genre and focus on areas where it has been innovative, helping create a crucially important sense of identity and a voice for the working classes sorely neglected through large swathes of literary history. But we are also setting out to make space for new voices to emerge, who can freely imagine Scotland's future as a diverse and hopeful nation.

As result of these lectures, talking to members of the audience and continuing research, a working definition of miserablism has emerged. This list is still being collated and will continue to be a work in progress.

The key characteristics of Scottish miserablism

- The main protagonist is a male tragic working-class hero, often a drifter and/or 'hard man' struggling with addiction. Alcohol, drugs, gambling, or violence are his 'fatal flaw'. The motivating theme (the emotional drive of the film) is a desire for 'order' or 'validation'.

- The younger hero is often a 'rites of passage' character who is ripped from childhood (often fatherless) and initiated into a world of chaos, crime and addiction.

- Unemployment and economic deprivation play key roles in the miserablist hero's motivation and the feeling that he has no choice.
- Uncompromising violence, physical and/or emotional, is part of the film's landscape/territory.
- The hero comes from a historically dysfunctional extended family and/or collapsed community.
- Secrets, lies, unforgiven misdeeds, a lack of redemption and the absence of hope within relationships characterise storylines in which the sins of the fathers are revisited upon their offspring.
- The influence and bleakness of the weather dominate the mise-en-scène, particularly darkness and rain.
- Women play secondary roles, often chastising the main protagonists and encouraging them to change, but to no avail. They generally function as either 'enablers' or as 'co-addicts', joining in with the protagonist's self-destructive lifestyle.
- Black humour is used to sweeten the bitter pill.
- The dialogue is 'street language' indigenous to its setting, usually a well-observed Scots vernacular, the vocabulary dense with expletives.
- Urban squalor and industrial wastelands prevail as exterior settings.
- Interior settings revolve around utilitarian domestic spaces and the pub.
- Guilt and unconsciously repressed religious values often inform the actions of both the protagonist and the antagonist – this is a Godless universe but it is dominated by a superstitious and punishing form of fate.
- A sense of worthlessness is generated by the idea that a 'superior' power has the upper hand, be it a gang, an addiction or another nation (inevitably, the English).
- The predominant style is naturalist informed by both the Scots Literary Naturalist tradition (James Kelman, William McIlvanney) and British Social Realist cinema (ie *Room at the Top* (1958), *Saturday Night and Sunday Morning* (1960)).
- A limited number of restricted locations and use of non-celebrity

actors mean that Miserablism lends itself to low-budget production, which makes it an exportable national product.

- There is no escape and no matter how hard a Scottish Miserablist hero tries he is doomed to failure. The only alternative is to leave Scotland and never come back. The message is that to survive or change the hero must live in exile, from which he can never return.

What tended to shock audiences most about miserablism was not only the negative message it articulates that change or hope seems impossible, but also its lack of answers, tools or solutions to the hero's problem. Across the canon, across the decades, there has been no real shift toward recovery or redemption. What started as an important protest movement that gave a 'real' voice to the poor and the oppressed has become horribly stuck.

CHAPTER ONE

Literary Roots: The Making of Miserablism

DAVID MANDERSON

I'VE LIVED IN GLASGOW all my life, except for four years at university in St Andrews and two years when I travelled abroad in Europe, Canada and the States as the roadie for the folk band The Tannahill Weavers. I left Scotland in 1979 shortly after the referendum, coming back only periodically, not long enough to see what was really going on. When I quit the road and returned to Glasgow for good in 1982 it felt as if the place had fundamentally changed. I was 24, unemployed and signing on, and it seemed as if the whole world had ground to a halt. Up and down Byres Road shops were selling things I'd never imagined anyone would want to buy – telephones, for example. And there were wine bars, strange looking new places hung with foliage and with windows you could see into instead of the narrow frosted vents of the old pubs. But the makeover hadn't made things better. The streets seemed empty, the lanes and alleyways vacant and there was a kind of coldness about the place I'd never seen before, a feeling that if you didn't have the money to go into the new-fangled places, you'd better move on. It was all very different from the rough and ready sameness that had dominated my home city before I'd left, where you'd always be made welcome provided you smoked, drank and looked like everyone else. The world had become divided between the haves and the have nots, and the indifference of the former towards the latter was the biggest new trend in town.

It felt then, and still feels, like more than my own experience. Scotland really did change at that time, spinning through several psychological and sociological revolutions or realisations, circling round and round itself as it tried to figure out what was going, all the while dancing, filled with hatred (and self-hatred), to Thatcher's tune.

It's now widely believed that Scotland's disenfranchisement after the referendum led to artistic freedom, but that wasn't apparent at the time. I was trying 'to be a writer', puzzling my way through short stories, finding the crushing boredom of the dole the last thing I needed for inspiration. I'd written well before I'd gone on my travels, unclear where I was going but struggling towards something. After I came back I started to write badly, dispiritedly, repetitively, without hope. I just couldn't see a way out. The trap I was in wasn't just having no money and no prospects – it was of having no existence. I'd been rubbed out of whatever picture was supposed to be there, dropped from the plan, and what was worse was that I couldn't seem to see myself among the explosion of arts events that were taking place around me. The posters on streetlights and in café windows studded with the names of new playwrights and poets had nothing to do with me. The mind-numbing emptiness of eking out time on benefits increased the sensation of not really being there, the phantom on other people's streets.

The world moved on, changing more rapidly than I ever thought it could. But all down the years that feeling of everything belonging to someone else never left. It's a long-term scar of unemployment that I share, no doubt, with many others, and it has had the miserablist effect of making it easy to believe that nothing can ever really change, that the bad times will return no matter what, that there's no way out. What's the point of struggling on when there's no prospect of change, even though change is everywhere? Fatalism in Scottish politics and culture is still one of its strongest characteristics – although successive SNP administrations have done something to alleviate the feeling that nothing can ever get better – and it's strongest of all in the arts. It's an insistent negativity that accuses things of being the way they are because they always have been. There isn't any choice. It's just the way things are. And hell mend you if you're agin it.

The thing called miserablism in this book is this force, and it's a double-edged blade that sometimes cuts through the bullshit and sometimes cuts us. It's capable of making us – by whom I mean anyone who lives in Scotland or has Scottish connections and lives abroad or shares the Scots' 'sensibility of the mind' – able to speak out in a special way, a powerful and uncompromising manner that can sometimes change things. At other times it keeps us silent and keeps us down. It's a special blend of pessimism, darkness, stubbornness, moral questioning and fatalism that can be both one of the most implacable enemies of tyranny and a tyrant itself. At its best it bursts forth in amazing flights of revolutionary fervour. It helps us identify lies and injustice, makes us feel that we have the right and the power to attack them, and has given Scottish writing at certain points a particularly strong blend of politics and aesthetics, as distinct and strong a tang in its arts and its life as peat-smoked whisky. It can bloom into flame because we're still ruled by governments hundreds of miles away that know very little about us and care less, trying to scare us into compliance when they feel they have something to lose if we leave them, but it's also very Scottish, part of who we are. At its worst, it makes us acquiescent and compliant and ensures we mind our place. Like a bad teacher it prevents us from believing in ourselves and from celebrating our existence. It's also the bit of us where we're never to blame. We didn't have a hand in empire, we were colonised without our complicity, it's all 'the English's' fault. It can be bold, courageous, proud and capable of great resistance, and it can be appallingly self-destructive. It's a cultural shield that has kept Scottish identity intact, up to a point. It's also kept it down, stopping it from getting above itself or thinking that it's got any right to walk in the sun. It's the cast of mind that thinks Scotland is great and that we've made a huge contribution to world affairs, science, the arts and history but will vote No in the forthcoming referendum, fear conquering bravemouth bravado in the end. It's intimately connected with our social hierarchies where Power isn't just Might, Power is Right, and the latter-day miserablist hero, now that vital battles in Scottish arts over language and politics have been won by other people, is its great representative, someone we know well from a thousand books, plays and films. He walks through the pages of our written and screen fiction, especially in film and television, every day. But we pay him far more respect than he's due. His time has gone. He was only one of a number of possible heroes anyway and he's no longer at the forefront of their ranks. He's toast, yesterday's news. And it's high time we gave him the push.

Miserablism in Scottish fiction goes back a long way. Its origins are probably in Calvinism, as Cairns Craig argues in *The Modern Scottish Novel*, along with other ideals like the rejection of fancy statues and saints in preference for plain old realism. Like Calvinism or any other dominant religion, miserablism is certain that things can't be any other way. Ordinariness, uniformity and not giving yourself airs and graces above your station are its markers, milestones along the humble path to paradise. Individuality, sticking your neck out and being ambitious are frowned on. Everybody must be the same as everyone else – though some are better than others, of course – as we have been on earth and ever shall be in heaven. Plainness, an insistence on reality and intolerance for alternatives are always its characteristics.

But miserablism and Calvinism aren't the same thing, though they're often assumed to be. Calvinism was not just an ideology but also a highly practical way of thinking, modeled less on fundamentalism than the idea of the community, and it contained a fair degree of tolerance within its ideal of the self-sustaining society. The Presbyterian tenant farmer, with his Bible, his two-room cottage, one for the family and one for the beasts, his tiny garden and his cabbage patch might seem a bit of a dour type to us today, but he was no fire-eating fanatic and no outcast. He didn't suffer any particular addiction, and his motivating desire was not order or validation because he already possessed them. His family was settled and his community was intact, although it suffered during times of famine and deprivation like any other peasant society. And he knew exactly where he stood with God and the devil. The most important thing to him was the shared values of his culture at the heart of his agrarian society. Provided he kept his feet on the ground and his heart pure of idolatry, sin or any Popish nonsense, his soul could be saved.

But deep within this relatively humane way of thinking (although little about Calvinism could be called cheerful), was the darkest of dark concepts – the idea of predestination, or Antinomianism. Many within the community openly or, as the Kirk gradually drove it underground, secretly believed that some (themselves) would be saved no matter what they did on this earth, while everyone else would be damned. It was a heresy banned after much debate but it clung on within religious outlook like a bad cold, never quite shaken off and hidden within its system. It simply wasn't possible to unpick this idea from the rest of the ideology – it was buried somewhere in there among all the finer values of sharing, caring and improving, and it ran deep in the Scottish psyche and the established, communal way of doing things. Robert Burns's *Holy Willie's Prayer* accurately satirises the mealy-mouthed hypocrisy of the malicious neighbour who attributes all merit to himself and none to others:

> Yet I am here, a chosen sample,
> To show thy grace is great and ample:
> I'm here, a pillar 'o Thy temple,
> Strong as a rock,
> A guide, a buckler, and example
> To a' Thy flock!

Jealous and bigoted, spiteful and bitterly resentful of anyone more free-spirited, truly mean in his actions and his thoughts, Holy Willie is at the heart of his society, a respected member of the Kirk but also a secret force lurking within it, seeking to wrestle control from others and rule long after the height of Calvinist domination has passed. Burns was no miserablist but he knew miserablism well, and spent a good deal of his life and his writing heading in the opposite direction.

The chilling idea that the Elect can be saved but that most are destined for hell is the Scottish take on fanaticism. Both it and the miserablist cast of writing defined by this book have been strong in this small nation. They're both absolute ways of looking at things, they're both concerned with the real world as opposed to other ways of showing it, they both refuse the possibility of redemption and they are both, by and large, to do with men. Predestination might seem like a long time ago, but modern writers such as Hector MacMillan (whose play *The Sash*, with its central figure of the sectarian Orangeman, was recently revived) and Liz Lochhead (whose *Mary Queen of Scots Got Her Head Chopped Off* portrays John Knox as 'woman's arch-enemy) agree that the influence of Calvinism has been profound on contemporary Scottish affairs and in the formation of Scottish gender. One does not cast out a religious way of thinking by ceasing to believe in god, especially not one rooted in a shared sense of history, society and 'common sense'. The point where artistic expression and the predetermined (meaning what can never change) meet, is uniquely Scottish and is the wellspring of miserablism.

This isn't to say that all dark realistic Scottish stories – thrillers, crime fiction, literary fiction, the work of Alan Sharp and James Kelman, 'Social Realism' and so on – are miserablist. Some of them use black humour to sweeten the pill and Scots vernacular for very different effects. The unemployed hard man ripped from his childhood need not finish his story in an inescapable situation, although he usually does in the Scottish tradition. And it doesn't make all miserablist texts bad, far from it. Why shouldn't any culture have many different kinds of stories, some of them dark, depressing, difficult and urgently trying to tell us something about trapped men? Indeed, miserablist fiction is vital at certain times. When things are dark, difficult and disempowering – which has been the case many times in Scotland and no doubt will be again – we need the angry working-class male hero, torn from his family, cast out from the rest of society, his community in collapse, struggling with his addictions and often violent, to spit out what he sees more clearly than the rest of us. He shows us ourselves because he stands apart, making us 'see ourselves as others see us'. More than once it's been these angry, outspoken, radical words in different varieties of rich, earthy Scots from the street or the field that have opened our eyes to the way we really are, especially over the last 30 or so years. But it's the contention here that after his first and most effective impact, the miserablist hero and his world are copied in the work of his admirers until they're pale shadows of their former selves, but set in stone to keep those who make them in power. When he and his dark world are invoked time and again for no better reason than to make us feel unhappily stuck in a grim hopeless place, just because we're supposed to have a dark male hero in our novels, films and plays who insists, as he always does, that all stories should be about Him, he has nothing left to say.

The miserablist texts mentioned here are sometimes the first ones, not always low points in our literature and sometimes their opposites. Some of these texts signalled the start of a change, sometimes for the better. None, however, offered solutions. Change is impossible in the miserablist tale. A story about an inescapable state of being can't offer a way out. There may be moments of lightness or comedy or even faint whimpers of hope, but the point is to end in a place from which there can be no escape.

In the Enlightenment era Scottish writers and thinkers invented rational arguments to advance new ideas of intellectual liberty, and in the Romantic age they invented dramatic tales of adventure to tap into the new sense of personal freedom. The poets and novelists of early 19th-century Scottish Romanticism returned especially to the past to plunder it for myths, legends and tales of the amazing courage and gruesome torture of the martyrs, recasting the old days in new kinds of stories like the epic poem or the latest fad, the novel. The first signs of miserablism were foreshadowed in one of the best-known books of the era. James Hogg, secretly, and keeping well away from his 'friends' and fellow writers as he did it, wrote possibly the world's first psychological thriller in the now renowned *The Private Memoirs and Confessions of a Justified Sinner*. There can be no more wretched a protagonist than Robert Wringhim, fatally split by his delusions, his past and even his birth, haunted by a double who may be real or may be a hallucination, driven to a shameful death without redemption, his grave violated and his corpse torn apart by callous gentleman grave robbers. But he is not the only miserablist hero in the tale. His brother George, his opposite in every way, who frequents the inns, brothels and street riots of the Scottish capital, is also a dark character addicted to his chosen lifestyle, capable of great violence and inexorably pinned to his fate. Robert is a tragic hero whose fate is apparent from the moment he meets his nemesis in the shape of Gilmartin and fails to see who he is. He is ripped from his childhood through having no birthright and initiated into a world of chaos and crime because of the nature of the beliefs handed down to him. Secrets, lies and unforgiven deeds haunt his family, and his real father's blessings leads him into his fatal error. Even the devil has miserablist tendencies, being fated to take on the appearance of whoever he deals with and seeming to share his victims' torments. The rich vernacular of the servants and labourers is contrasted with the much more mannered, and false, English of the middle classes, and prostitution, betrayal and murder infest the squalor of the Old Town. Miserablism is part of the psychosis portrayed by the book and part of the psyche of a nation deeply and increasingly divided by language, internal colonialism and above all, as Hogg knew better than anyone, by class (for an insight into the writer's circumstances as he wrote the book, see Peter Garside's introduction to the Stirling/South Carolina 2002 edition of *The Confessions*). It is also explicitly linked to predestination. And it is one of the main reasons for the very real terror created by the book.

But *The Confessions* is also more than a miserablist work. Hogg's characters are complex, their existences evoked with sorrow and pity as well as anger, while true miserablism requires tears knuckled from the corner of an eye as life defeats the hero yet again, his emotions driven back where they belong beneath the surface of a hard masculine exterior, usually by strong drink. It's part of *The Confessions* startling nature that it is a Romantic work, a Gothic one, a supernatural thriller and a work of Calvinism all at once, as well as an early precursor of miserablism.

Miserablism is really a 20th-century phenomenon, but it is related to another movement that preceded it – the 'Kailyard' school of Scottish fiction. This succession of highly popular novels written at the end of the 19th century with rural or small-town settings was later thought so parochial, sickly sweet and sentimental in their picture of backwater life that it was held responsible for a deterioration of Scottish writing, and even accused of killing it off. Miserablism can be seen in some ways as a reaction to the Kailyard. The writings of J. M. Barrie, S. R. Crockett and Ian Maclaren did not really constitute a school, and ranged widely over matters of morals and manners, small-town affairs, humorous misunderstandings, historical events and passionate evangelism. Nostalgia was ever present, but it was not necessarily vapid, and sometimes expressed a genuine sense of loss. George, one of Drumtochty's successful scholars, who graduated from the teacher Domshie's village school to go to theUniversity of Glasgow in Maclaren's *Beside the Bonnie Brier Bush*, returns home to die:

> When George came home for the last time, Marget went back and forward all afternoon from his bedroom to the window, and hid herself behind the laburnum to see his face as the cart stood before the stile. It told her plain what she had feared, and Marget passed through her Gethsemane with the gold blossoms falling on her face...

Beside the Bonnie Brier Bush might not show a dark hero battling things out, condemned to stay in his current state forever, but it isn't the box of soft-centred chocolates it's supposed to be either. The Kailyard novels can be accused with some accuracy of being backward looking and having little to do with the reality of most people's lives, but they chimed with large sections of the book reading public at home and among the Scottish diaspora, not because the sense of loss and change in them referred to a mythical twilit past, but because the loss was recent. The Kailyard movement was really a response to the huge social changes of the Industrial Revolution, which were probably calamities and which Tom Devine describes in terms of the ebbs and flow of internal population movements and emigration. But even within their own era these books were being identified as springing from the cabbage patch, and as a problem that needed addressing. 'Kailyard' was to become a label for any kind of Scottish writing thought to be hackneyed. Rhona Brown of the University of Glasgow has written of the way the term has come to be bandied about until it has virtually lost any meaning. And these pieces of writing, no matter how valid or invalid they were, had run their course by the end of the 19th century. Another force was gathering even before they had dispersed. Miserablism was about to be born.

George Douglas Brown's *The House with the Green Shutters* (1901) savaged this light school of literature. There are no open references to it, but at the book's opening a well-kent picture of dawn in a Scottish small town lulls the reader into believing that this will be another sentimental tale:

> The freshness of the air, the smoke rising thin and far above the red chimneys, the sunshine glistening on the roofs and gables, the rosy clearness of everything beneath the dawn, above all the quietness and peace, made Barbie, usually so poor to see, a very pleasant place to look down at...

But soon it's clear *The House with the Green Shutters* will be a very different sort of story:

> Gourlay smiled, grimly, and a black gleam shot from his eye...

The House with the Green Shutters deliberately and consciously breaks with Kailyard conventions. The setting is a small village with a local cast of characters, but it is a picture of people in a place and a time that is dark, foreboding and malign. The struggle for power is between John Gourlay and his competitors but it is clear from early in the book that Gourlay's plans for himself and his family are doomed. A grandly dark tale with strong gothic elements is acted out, describing a decline inevitable from the start, all the more ironic for being set in a tiny inward-looking world. The story's outcome is foreshadowed and inexorable in its consequences, its main events echoed mockingly or insinuatingly by a chorus of lazy, malicious villagers, the Bodies. The older and the younger John Gourlay, his son, are fatally split in terms of temperament. The father's strength and courage seem to suck those qualities from his son, who is weak, lonely and imaginative. In Edinburgh, unwillingly attending college, the younger Gourlay becomes addicted to alcohol. The older Gourlay's desire for validation in his home town of Barbie, to be a man of standing and the greatest person in the town, is his main motive. The younger John's rites of passage are determined by his father, forcing the son towards his destruction, and he is pushed into his course of addiction and crime by the older man's pitiless drive towards social improvement. Violence flares with the increasing threat of economic deprivation as Gourlay's fruitless ambition leads him into one mistake after another. The bodies spend their days delighting in Gourlay's mistakes, taking small-minded, petty revenge for his self-importance. Their malicious slander seems to indicate a community in a kind of moral collapse, and also one in the middle of change as the coming of the railway, new mines and new commercialism transform the village's fortunes and the balance of power. Mrs Gourlay and her daughter Janet are pushed into secondary roles, the mother's love for her son crushed by her husband's contempt for him. Fate is punishment, meted out in a far worse form than Gourlay ever deserves. It is a remorseless story of a family's total destruction.

There's no doubt that Brown's famous novel returned to Scottish writing a power that had been lacking from it during the Kailyard era, and perhaps since the era of Scott and Hogg. It also effectively ended the Kailyard movement by overturning its conventions. It was to be the book most Scottish Modernist writers, many of them miserablists, looked to after the First World War and picked up from. From the time of its publication, it became possible again to write dark, brooding fiction about Scottish life. The lack of any possibility of redemption was the point, and what gave the book its impact. *The House with the Green Shutters*, and also John MacDougall Hay's *Gillespie* (1914) – both much less commercially successful than the books by the Kailyard authors –had a much more slow-burning and long-term impact, at first difficult to gauge. They aligned Scottish writing not with a longed-for past but a bleak and inescapable future, socially and psychologically. It was a state of fictional affairs that was to last.

The period during the First World War is not known as one of the high points of Scottish writing, retreating in its poetry to rural affairs (as in

Hamewith by Charles Murray), or taking up positions in the trenches in the poetry of Joseph Lee and Ewart Alan MacIntosh. There were, however, signs that miserablism was becoming the norm. Patrick McGill's *The Rat-Pit* (1915) describes slum conditions in Glasgow from the point of view of one who'd really been there. His portrait of the filthy tenements and 'warm middens', and their maze-like, inescapable nature was probably the most first-hand of many descriptions of the Glasgow slums in the early 20th century, as Moira Burgess has outlined. In the same year it was Richard Hannay's duty not to be a miserablist about things himself (in fact he's annoyingly cheerful and determined to make a jolly good show of things) but to enforce miserablist conditions on others, and to be part of a miserablist form, in *Mr Standfast*, John Buchan's third thriller or 'shocker'. Employed as a spy in the service of King and Empire, Hannay's job is to visit centres of possible depravity at home, flush out shirkers and infiltrate the spy ring they naively shelter. He visits the homes of conscientious objectors, artists' villages and the tenement flats of striking shipyard workers. His quest is to keep things as they are, to ensure that nothing disturbs the war effort through surveillance. The grinding repression of the state, for all Hannay's steely pleasantry, is clear. Miserablism here is government-enforced, an existence rather than a living, a state of being on a war footing in a city clamped into entrenched, reinforced positions, its subordination policed by males. Young men are to be parted from their families, their addictions encouraged. Violent confrontation is proof of manliness, and any inclination towards peace an unhealthy deviance. Women are pushed so far into the background, they disappear. Urban squalor and industrial wastelands prevail, necessary parts of an imperialist whole with no silly little upstart nationalism allowed. Buchan's picture of Glasgow during the war is the precursor of later miserablist texts such as *No Mean City* and the stereotype of Glasgow that derived from it, which in many ways is still with us and has had so much to do with the destructive influence of the miserablist hero in Scottish films and television. Part of the stereotype is the physical fight, repressed rage bursting through the thin veneer of civilisation, and in this version uniformed surveillance adds to the tension. It's probably a faithful portrait of the mood of the time as Hannay visits Glasgow and is at first surprised by the number of able-bodied men on the streets (the suspicion that any man not in khaki may be a coward or a traitor is evident from the opening page), only to remember the city's shipbuilding and munitions industries. He treads carefully up a tenement stair, 'for like all South Africans I have a horror of dirt'. He attends a public debate where some of the presenters, probably spies, demand peace. A fight breaks out between them, the plain-clothes policemen who are keeping them under watch and some loyal soldiers. It is a glimpse of the grim city stretching back to Poe and Baudelaire and the figure of the *flaneur*, the subversive wanderer, the spy in the crowd at the heart of Modernity, but it is a specifically Scottish version, following the same thread of the male trapped in his predestined position that Hogg had foreshadowed and George Douglas Brown had begun. But here, it is encouraged, part of the war effort, and it comes in one of the earliest thrillers, a form which by its very nature conventionally pitches good and evil against each other, and so tended to encourage miserablism in the 20th century.

Mr Standfast also identified the figure of the West of Scotland Hard Man in the miserablist syndrome, the bruiser who was to carry violence forward on his feet and fists for much of the 20th century. As Hannay fights one of the patriotic soldiers, so as to appear to the 'conshies' like a potential member of the spy ring, his heart leaps at the sight of the 'broad, thickset fellow, of the adorable bandy-legged stocky type that I had seen go through the Railway Triangle at Arras as though it were blotting paper.' Broad, thickset, violent Glaswegians would later make a crucial contribution to the miserablist genre, well beyond Scotland. They were the easiest stereotype to introduce to screen dramas or other kinds of fiction a superficial sense of 'conflict', 'suspense' or 'tension' in drama, and they still are.

The slaughter of a generation during the First World War by tanks, artillery and machine guns proved beyond doubt that machines could outdo men – the Depression proved there would be nothing for them on their return. *Dismembering the Male* by Joanna Bourke describes the way these factors shored up rather than destroyed the masculine myth. This would have been as true in Scotland as anywhere, but perhaps more so considering the huge sacrifice of their young men made by the industrial towns of the Central Belt. The transfer of the Scottish miserablist hero from the small rural town of *The House with the Green Shutters* to the urban environment devastated by war, with the violent miserablist male now in control, was confirmed in another archetypal work. *No Mean City*, published in 1935, followed the career of Johnny Stark the 'Razor King' in the Gorbals slums of the '20s, his life and loves in single ends, filthy closet beds and stair-heids, and his battles with the rival gangs of Plantation and Townhead. The book portrayed Glasgow in a way it has never been able to shake off. The sons, wives and daughters of unemployed, drunken workers, and maimed ex-soldiers with nothing to do but work in menial jobs or loaf the streets, fill the same slums as *Mr Standfast*, their boredom punctuated by bouts of drinking, violence and sex. They dream of escape and fail to find it. The Scottish Hard Man and the grim city come together in a way to show that these are the lost souls, the damned. There is no way out for any of them, only acceptance of their condition, or death. Two characters, the gangster McLatchie and John Gray, beaten by Stark in fights, slink from the town, but their leaving is part of their punishment, a particularly shameful one. Neither the Razor King nor his brother Peter nor Bobbie Hurley the dancer escape their fates. Women appear only in secondary roles. Mary Hay is Johnny Stark's would-be chastiser at 'the sherricking', until a blow to her jaw and a kick in her ribs knock her out, while Lizzie becomes his co-addict in his life of criminality. Both these women's relationships, with Johnny Stark and with later partners, are without hope, while Johnny's life follows the same drunken, brawling trajectory as his father's. Hosts of imitators were to follow the lead set by authors Alexander McArthur and H. Kingsley Long, and theirs was to be the dominant image of unalleviated violence and poverty that hung over Glasgow for decades, and still does in the minds of many people who've never been there. Johnny Stark meets every one of the conditions for the miserablist hero, from the idea of being ripped from childhood through poverty to the increasing addiction to alcohol which is his eventual downfall. So miserablism may be literary, as in *The House with the Green Shutters*, or commercial, as in *No Mean City*, but in the case of Glasgow, the cliché has been so influential that it has formed an overwhelmingly miserablist picture of the real place. Other, later Glaswegian writers, some of them miserablists themselves, had to fight this against this image to salvage from it at least some impression of real people doing their best to live.

Miserablism wasn't necessarily limited to Scottish fiction. In 1925, with the publication of *Sangschaw*, Hugh MacDiarmid's lyrics transformed what was understood to be Scottish poetry, although it had continued to be practised by East Coast Scots poets Violet Jacob and Marion Angus. Always controversial, MacDiarmid stamped his identity on Scottish letters with *A Drunk Man Looks at the Thistle*, a revolutionary epic, consciously a polemic. His establishment of the anthology *Northern Numbers*, where known and established writers were gradually replaced by a new generation, placed him at the forefront of what was christened the Scottish Renaissance and the new wave of Scottish writers who were to rediscover and resurrect Scottish literature. He didn't invite this leadership, and in fact warned against it, but his contemporaries and compatriots – MacCaig, Goodsir Smith, MacKay Brown, Edwin Morgan, Garioch, Hamish Henderson – took inspiration from him, though they also disagreed with many of his stances. MacDiarmid made possible a vibrant new identity for Scottish writing in the 20th century, particularly through his invention of 'synthetic Scots', a consciously created version of a language which proved that a distinctly new but also historically-based 'tradition' could be invented, or be reborn. But his refusal to compromise meant he endured hardships that went beyond the extremes of poverty. He survived long periods of neglect and depression, and suffered a breakdown in Shetland in 1935. Rediscovered and eulogised by a second generation of writers in the post-war period, his satirical anger was sometimes mistaken for literal truth. And his complexity as a poet, the layers of meaning and inference on which he was calling, were frequently lost on audiences more intent on new fashions. His famously controversial diatribes, which were really all-out attacks on the establishment, led to apparent opposition to change in his later years that could make his influence on new Scottish writing seem thoroughly miserablist. In fact, MacDiarmid was anything but resistant to influence, and remains one of the most multi-faceted and open of all Scottish poets to new voices and ideas. This was despite the fact that he himself met many of the conditions for the miserablist hero. His life was full of hard times and poverty, which he shared with his family. The desire for order, in his case the re-establishment and renewal of the Scottish literary tradition into a new Renaissance, and his validation as a Great Poet, were his driving force and his open aim. Unemployment and economic deprivation played significant parts in his life and he regarded himself as coming from a collapsed, repressed nation (which Buchan's portrait of Glasgow in *Mr Standfast* tends to bear out), but one which, he believed, could remake and reinvent itself. His circle has been sometimes been accused of marginalising women, and Michael Gardiner has written of the importance of drinking and the pub to the group of Scottish male poets and writers who seemed to rule Scottish writing at this time. But in fact MacDiarmid was encouraging towards writers of all kinds, while obsessions with debates over rules about language, satirised by Tom Leonard in the poster that advertises a debate over the 'spellin o' this poster' was more the view of an insular Edinburgh bourgeoisie, who were only too happy to adopt views that excluded the majority of people (especially their cousins in the West), than of any practising poet, and was countered by later experimenters like Iain Hamilton Finlay and Edwin Morgan. The famous confrontation between the grand old poet and Alexander Trocchi at the 1962 Edinburgh Festival – supposedly a clash between old-fashioned rigidity and dynamic post-modernism – has overshadowed the fact that Trocchi admired MacDiarmid, recognising in him a restless refusal to accept the limits of conventional form. MacDiarmid was also often unjustly accused of tyrannising Scottish writing when in reality he was often helpful to younger poets, as Alan Bold points out in his biography. It was more his refusal to compromise and the scathing nature of his attacks than anything MacDiarmid ever wrote that made his later reputation miserablist, but that misleading image was a powerful one, and to some extent persists.

Miserablism in the first wave of the Scottish Renaissance came too in Edwin Muir's *Scottish Journey*, which travels the length of the land and finds it utterly still, gripped by powers it doesn't have any control over, and unknown to itself. This stunning portrait of a nation in the darkest time of economic depression, with the miniature slag-heaps of the Lanarkshire coal fields like a pygmy mockery of the Romantic landscapes, makes Scotland its own miserablist hero, orphaned, its community destroyed, its very identity a vacuum. It was a version of Scotland that had much to do with Muir's own experience of exile to Glasgow from his beloved Orkney, and the loss of many members of his family. Muir too was ripped from the world of his childhood. He saw plenty of chaos and crime around him, evidence of collapsed communities from which there was no escape, while urban squalor and the industrial wastelands horrified and fascinated him.

He took miserablism to the core of Scottish existence, seeing them as one and the same.

The Edinburgh Festival of 1962, where MacDiarmid and Alexander Trocchi, the Scottish writer of *Young Adam* and also editor of the *sigma* series of papers and collaborator with the leader of the Situationist International, Guy Debord, confronted each other has been viewed as a key moment, where the frozen form of miserablism that MacDiarmid, at that moment in his long poetic life, was identified with, started to crack. With a new surge of '60s optimism, it's argued, American influences in poetry and music, and a new generation intent on freedom and free love, change had arrived. But in reality change was imperceptible, and avant-garde ideas in music, poetry and the arts were far from central to most Scottish people's experiences, while Trocchi's *Young Adam* and *Cain's Book*, far from questioning miserablism, played on it in terms of their depictions of urban squalor, addiction and murder. Miserablism was not redundant in stories about real lives in an industrial urban environment only beginning to rust away. In Alan Sharp's *A Green Tree in Gedde*, John Moseby and Harry Gibbon discuss happiness in The Rowan Tree pub in Greenock. The concept annoys Moseby, who thinks that it doesn't apply, while Gibbon appears to feel he doesn't have it, but the predominant image is of a World War One soldier who suffocated himself in his own kitbag, a story Moseby has had from one of the pub regulars. In this miserablist novel, conflict, the feeling of being physically trapped and the inevitability of fate are strong elements again. Gibbon, in search of his sexuality, and the adventurous Cuffee leave Britain on a quest to find themselves by losing themselves. But the real adventure for all the characters in the book is interior, both spiritual and sexual, exploring forbidden places an older generation dared not go:

> ... and she could feel his hands on her back stroking down to cup and splay on her hips, run up her flanks and grip under the soft crutches of her armpits...

Women play subservient roles in this form of freedom, waiting at home to be released into their desire by wandering men, while Cuffee and Gibbon mostly fail in their quest. Sharp's point seems to be that those who leave find little while those who stay, personified by Moseby, find less. Moseby is illegitimate, rootless in a world where happiness seems irrelevant, trapped in a family which he ultimately loses anyway. His fatal flaw is his refusal to move on. His community, if not yet collapsed, is eroding as young people leave and those who remain seem like shell-shocked survivors, while the city is like the empty shell of a great liner:

> A pub was just opening, the barman putting back the concertina grille and looking once at the sky before going back inside. Moseby looked at the sky too, it was pale blue and shimmied with cloudings. He went in. The public bar had yellow varnished paneling.

Characters come together in couplings that have little to do with desire. 'Come on Johnny' says Cathie from the bed without opening her eyes when Moseby calls at her flat for a briefcase he has deliberately left behind. She is like 'an older, married sister', he thinks as he undresses to join her. He's repelled by his desires but has no choice in them:

> ... the awkward loll of the gross old neck, the features contorted in drunken, daylight sleep, the splayed knees, the stocking, the skin... Disgust and excitement uneasily blended.

Cuffee finds little more in the end than a severe case of concussion when he is attacked by two German girls. Ironically rescued by nuns after his proud sexual escapades, he returns home. 'He has changed', his girlfriend Gerda says, and this is Sharp's final comment on him. Gibbon and Ruth find their answers in intimacy, not in action. Any change there may have been has had no effect. Nothing has moved on and there is the over-whelming sensation of hope stifled, of suffocation in the kit-bag. Sharp himself left Scotland without completing the trilogy of which *A Green Tree in Gedde* was meant to be the first part (although the third part seems to have been reworked as the film *Night Moves*), moving to Hollywood where he became a successful writer of thrillers and westerns before returning to Scottish subjects with the film *Rob Roy* in 1996. *A Green Tree in Gedde*, like *The House with the Green Shutters*, is another work where miserablism dominates, showing us the reality of our predicament by making it clear that for folk like us, there's no way out. Things stay depressingly the same even when they look like they've changed, just like the narrator in Irvine Welsh's 'Eurotrash' and like Renton at the end of *Trainspotting*, who both think that leaving Scotland means escape:

> I took tram number 17 from Rab/Robbie's depressing little scheme in the western sector into the city centre. Nothing happens in the places like the one we stayed in... I could've been back in Wester Hailes... One dustbin for the poor outside of action strasser is much the same as any other, regardless of the city it serves...

Miserablist heroes always find their escape tunnel blocked off, or, more likely, a delusion in the first place, although, as we'll see in the next chapter, there's a gap in this miserablist psychogeography, an unknown, unexplained space between the extremes of the urban and the rural, which is exile, the stories of those who leave and can never come back. They can never return because miserablism allows no compromise of its conditions.

Archie Hind's Mat Craig in *The Dear Green Place* seems to have discovered a time to write and live, miraculously, in late '50s Glasgow. Giving up his job in a slaughterhouse seems to release him from the imprisonment of employment or poverty, but all his plans come to nothing as his writing loses its way and becomes ugly and senseless while the money runs out. Mat isn't addicted to alcohol and his community seems strong but there is no escape from his predicament. The city is changing, the old ways collapsing in the face of the new, the violence of the old tenements replaced by the establishment of the Health Service and social security. But Mat dreams of the territory beyond the borders of his class, of places where his reading and his artistic longings become part of who he is and not the preserve of the middle classes who fence them off:

> 'Do you like the paintings?'
> The young man was looking at Mat with an absent curiosity. He seemed to be asking the question not out of any real interest but in order to note dutifully the reactions of the philistine.

Mat has the talent and knowledge to talk almost equally with 'a poet, a stage actor... three painters and a BBC producer...' but his birthright, his background and his circumstances can never allow him to join them. He is ripped from his certainty and solidity with this father's death, and 'divided against himself' he tears up his own novel.

> 'Ye're nut on, laddie. Ye're on tae nothin'.'

... A harsh, ugly, contemptuous, slangy voice. This time he didn't look round, for it was his own voice, he had spoken aloud.

He kneels on the Govan Ferry vomiting out his hope, his life, his dreams, his disappointments and his life in the city 'cast in iron'. It is an appropriate end to his aspirations. Mat Craig is even more of a miserablist hero than Sharp's Moseby or Gibbon because for him there is never any opportunity to break free of the city or of his conditions. He is the writer who can't write, the fish that can't swim, the bird that never flew.

The Dear Green Place and *A Green Tree in Gedde*, nevertheless, also broke new ground. They were miserablist works that offered us new ways to see ourselves, examining the lives of young people as change touches them and passes them by through no fault of their own, unlike the more hackneyed 'grim city' miserablism – or 'urban Kailyard' as it's now sometimes called – that was by that point the standard in popular film and television. Unlike Johnny Stark, but like Harry Gibbon, Mat aspires to more than his established route in life. He questions why he can't be allowed to do what he wants and sets out to find it. He fails, of course, but that's the point. Failure is the only possible outcome in miserablist fiction.

William McIlvanney's characters Docherty and Dan Scoular are two ends of a spectrum of decline in Graithnock, an Ayrshire mining town, in the novels *Docherty* and *The Big Man*. Proud, isolated and independent, embodying in his small frame all the courage and strength of his community, the only thing Docherty the miner has left by his death is his indomitable belief in protecting other people, the last redeeming feature in a dark picture of dwindling hope and opportunity. The warm, gritty community of Graithnock declines year after year as war, unemployment and increasing economic deprivation strip it further and further of its health. The community is beginning to collapse by the book's end. By the time we come to Dan Scoular's time in the '80s, the miserablist hero has come into his own. Graithnock is afflicted by decades of unemployment and squalor, personified by Scoular himself, a wild, undisciplined, addicted brawler who can only drift through life, from fight to fight, his only skill a big punch. His relationship is in danger, his children seem as if they will soon be fatherless, and there are no signs of redemption, only further disaster, ahead. The town, like him, is purposeless and lost, its meaning long gone.

He almost seems to escape his fate at the end of that book, protected by the last vestiges of his community, but his death at the hands of vengeful, violent gangsters is reported in the later McIlvanney novel *Strange Loyalties*. The punishing god of fate gets him in the end.

Part of the reason why miserablist characters and events seemed so powerful in Scottish writing of the '60s, '70s and '80s was that they were true. The authors knew the places they were based on and drew them from the life, and they were places, people and lives mostly excluded from British fiction. These male writers made important contributions to literature by placing authenticity of Scottish place and experience at the heart of their work and by making it clear why that was important to the rest of the world. It was always their intention to show things as they were. James Kelman's *The Bus Conductor Hines* and his short stories in *Not Not While the Giro* took these achievements even further. His trapped male characters suffer or exist or have a good time in spite of everything, their existences truncated, limited and subordinate to employers or the buroo but still jubilantly or angrily defiant, if only – or especially – in their imaginations. Kelman took miserablism further than any of his precursors, perhaps as far as it can go, but he has sometimes been unjustly accused of perpetuating its worst aspects. In fact, he demonstrated that this kind of writing could depict meaningful existences in new ways. But he still could not offer an alternative to the miserablist condition because he was showing, and he still shows, that it was real, it was true. Irvine Welsh introduced a wave of what could be mistaken for optimism in *Trainspotting*'s (1996) mix of house music, drugs and black humour, but in reality miserablism still ruled okay, his 'vernacular spectacular' a fireworks display that celebrated the end of the Thatcher era with great energy but achieved it through the tried and tested formula of disenfranchised males, urban squalor, punishing fate and black humour.

So the miserablist hero in Scottish literature has been one of its most important and courageous harbingers of new kinds of imaginative freedom. He's also been, in a thousand books, films and television programmes a figure of the greatest crassness who has lived down to his stereotype beyond even the most rudimentary elements of characterisation. The great miserablist achievements in Scottish literature, some of which have been described above, have been followed by their coarsening as lesser writers, interested only in the fame or the money and incapable of anything original, jumped on the gravy-train, especially after Scottish art took off and became trendy in or around 1980. There was never any possibility of these second-rate writers doing anything new – they weren't even trying. Kelman, Sharp, Hind and others did the hard work by breaking the ground. When the time came to cash in, what could be easier for their imitators than to place the Hard Man with his trapped existence permanently in the centre of the new territory, and keep him there?

He's still acting Hard when it's all over. No longer fashionable, his community having gone through many periods of boom and bust, with new kinds of wealth and squalor all around him, he's still behaving like nothing's changed. He was never even all that Hard in the first place, he was just pretending. Today he might wear an Armani suit, own a nightclub and a string of racehorses and quaff champagne, but he's still the same, still around, the same old bully. The children sheltering in their bedrooms, the wife weeping in the kitchen, the colleagues at the other desks, the brother trying to live his life a different way, the cousin whose grandparents moved abroad two generations ago, they all have their stories too, and free of him they could tell new ones about love or death or history or space travel or… anything really. But the miserablist hero won't have this. There are no other stories while he's still there. There's only One Way, His Way. The only True is his True. There's been a murrdurr and that's just the way it is.

We're all doomed. Doomed, I tell ye!

CHAPTER TWO

The Urban versus the Rural and Nothing in Between

DAVID MANDERSON

EVERYONE KNOWS we live in castles or tenements. There are no other Scotlands, nothing other than them and nothing in between. We have them in our literature, our portraits, our television and films and our music, so they must be true. Sometimes something comes along to stir this picture up a bit, but it doesn't last. We are after all the place of duality, of conflicting opposites, antisyzygic to the core, the land 'whaur extremes meet', as MacDiarmid said.

Again, much of it goes back to Walter Scott. Romantic Scotland – where we all live in castles – wasn't invented solely by him, but he had much to do with it. Later, when people got sick of the image, he took the lion's share of the blame, by which time it had degenerated to tea-towel history. But the fact that the tail end of Romanticism was a pale shadow of its origins doesn't make its beginnings false or limp. They were strong, radical and original in their day. Ossian, later vilified as a 'false' construct (as if a poet needs to carry credentials to establish his authenticity) drew on existing Gaelic verse to pull together his epics, reassembling something that could be remade from the remnants of his culture. The tartans that Scott dressed his archers and attendants in (and even the monarch himself), at the 1822 pageant, were not invented for that event as those seeking to portray the celebration as a work of complete fiction would have it. They were not solely created by Scott's fertile imagination and therefore 'false' (thus questioning Scotland's right to historical distinctiveness and self-determination), but had been in existence for some time before it, possibly centuries. It used to be argued, and sometimes still is by writers examining Scott's influence on Scottish culture during and after his lifetime, such as Stuart Kelly in *Scott-land*, that Scott invented Scotland at the Edinburgh pageant in order to sell it to the Empire. He did invent much of it, but his intention was always to renew and promote Scottish identity as distinct, both within and beyond imperialism, and it was a love he carried into his writing and his life. And his stage management of the celebration was successful, hugely so. Whatever danger there was of the disappearance of the Scottish nation evaporated in the face of the most successful national re-launch there has ever been, which was to last in military tradition, the arts and cultural events right up to today, promoting Scottish identity to a huge international audience.

But it meant that as far as the rest of the world was concerned we all lived in castles among sublime landscapes, or near them. This memory was to spread overseas with the emigration, forced or otherwise, of hundreds of thousands of families most of whom did indeed leave the rural rather than the urban behind, one that was remembered and treasured and passed down the generations along with their accents, customs and language.

The Industrial Revolution saw a dramatic convulsion of the whole Scottish population, with the rapid rise of the cities and the mining, processing and textile industries across the Central Belt and the emptying of the countryside. It wasn't just the Highlands that were cleared. The Borders too suffered a dramatic displacement of its people, and is still desolate compared to the rest of the country. 'Improvement' in farming and manufacturing methods hastened the process. Hogg was to complain of the change in relationship between the farmer and his servants and labourers, the working men and women who took up employment on the Scottish farms who had once shared their evening meal with their master and now fared for themselves in out-houses and barns. In fact Hogg in his lesser known writings – his memoirs, letters, tales and novels – demonstrates that the difference between the two worlds, the rural and the urban, wasn't as much of a dramatic schism as our artistic traditions were beginning to make us believe. He of all the writers of his time repeatedly crossed the barriers between urban and rural, wealthy and poor, Highland and Lowland, and, always lively and curious, recorded what he saw, even topics like cliffs full of sea-birds or strange visions dreamed after too much whisky that his peers deemed unsuitable for literature. His writing offers a much more nuanced, subtle and detailed picture of the various arts and parts of Scottish society and the way they were knitted together, than the now famous divisions.

The fissure in our arts between the castles of our imagination and the tenements of our reality was reinforced by the fault-line between Highland and Lowland, Highlanders enduring starvation and clearance throughout the 19th century at the same time as their landscape was being 'consumed' by tourists. Tom Devine has demonstrated, from his study of Scotland's contribution to the British Empire, that the areas of the Highlands which became the most depopulated were those where the regiments recruited most heavily, the image of the Highlander warrior, along with the threat of hunger, being used to persuade the younger generations during the Clearances that paid employment and some sort of future lay with the army rather than at home. The division between declining Highland or island paradise and overpowering urban squalor was also brought out in the work of Edwin Muir and Gaelic writers such as Neil Gunn in his novel *The Drinking Well*. The homeland left behind is a memory of gentleness and love, and the city a vision of hell where the Highlander must live and work, leading to physical deprivation and mental breakdown. This was no doubt true for many and an accurate picture of the turmoil and division of their lives, but it was to leave behind a trace in Scottish culture that echoed long through its film and literature, longer than its reality and never completely clear cut in the first place.

Even when we lived in the city, we were good at saying we lived in the country. Landscape paintings were displayed in the panoramas in Edinburgh in the 19th century, huge oils of the sublime mountains of the Trossachs and Glencoe hung in great rooms so the crowds wandering between them could feel as if they were walking among the peaks. This was carried into theatrical scene painting seen by mass audiences in the popular theatres. The galleries and theatres weren't far from the seething slums with their vennels and closes which were really open sewers, but the image of castles preserved throughout the Romantic era and beyond it the belief of 'true' Scotland as being a place of magnificence and gran-deur, the 'land of the mountain and the flood', and of the Highland dignity and courage that was bred there. Landseer's *Monarch of the Glen*, later the most despised representation of Victorian Balmorality, summed it all up, the great creature surveying the spectacle around him, surrounded by the misty mountains, an image that was ultimately used as an advertisement for Pears Soap. The golds, oranges, purples and browns of the landscape made a visual palette that passed directly into film, where Scott's stories, exported wholesale during the 19th century, became the most adapted of any Scottish novelist's in the 20th. But it was by now more than one man's work. It was a tradition, an argument, a discourse familiar to people who had no connection with Scotland and no need of one. Spectacle, colourful action, courageous deeds, exotic locations and adventure were just the right ingredients for a medium seen all over the world, and not just by the Scottish diaspora.

The change from the country to the dark urban community, in this case the small town, came, as we've seen, with the end of the Kailyard movement in literature. It rather unfairly bore the brunt of the hostility for everything that had gone before it with the publication of *The House with the Green Shutters* in 1901. But the new image evolved much more gradually in film. The reason was that films were made and sold internationally, and audiences, many of them Scottish, were willing to pay to see romantic stories set in the Highlands, buying into the 'castles and mountains' notion and probably rather proud, no matter what the real circumstances of their lives were, of the international impact of the Scottish tradition. Another reason was that film narrative takes the most spectacular images and dramatic moments from a story and freezes them into relatively simple structures, altering them wherever possible from narrative to visual. The result is not necessarily simplistic but, since a film is shorter than a novel, the original must be boiled down to its essentials and then cut in some way. The Hollywood tradition uses the simplest structure of all, reducing stories to narrative blocks where dramatic contrast is most effective. So well into the 20th century, although it was no longer the fashion in literature, colourful swashbuckling films about the Highlands or bizarre variations of Romantic Scotland were still being made, such as *Bonnie Prince Charlie* (1948), *Brigadoon* (1954), *The Three Lives of Thomasina* (1963), and Walt Disney's *Rob Roy, the Highland Rogue* (1953), although adaptations of Scott's stories began to tail off from about the '40s.

In literature during and after the First World War, as Buchan's *Mr Standfast* shows, the city started to become the dominant location, a particularly grim version of a named urban environment, the black tenements of Glasgow. *No Mean City* was the ultimate expression of another Scotland to rival the Romantic one, a more than equal and opposite force to it, and modernist writers, not all of them miserablists, attacked the Romantic version by stressing the other extreme. This had the effect, as ever in the land of dualities, of polarising our artistic places. We no longer lived in castles, we all lived in the Gorbals, and a grim hand-to-mouth struggle it was too. With the birth of the modernist Scottish film movement (christened Clydesidism) in industrialist films like *Floodtide* (1949), the cinematic world also became divided between the tradition of the urban versus the rural. These extremes weren't necessarily false in themselves, but they did tend to exclude other kinds of story. Constantly at war, constantly in opposition, they petrified – it seemed forever – the two versions of Scotland that were coming into existence during the Industrial Revolution and Walter Scott's and James Hogg's lifetimes (they died within a few years of each other, and the best of the Scottish Romantic movement went with them).

The urban side of this duality is a grimy, gritty maze with no connection to the sublime. The city in all its forms in modernity, symbolically and in reality, is intricately connected with the movement of the crowd and a feeling of isolation or detachment in it. TS Eliot's crowds sway across London Bridge in *The Waste Land*, while 20th century forms like the thriller stalk the alleyways and mean streets, although they might take to the hills in flight or to avoid capture, as Richard Hannay does in *The Thirty Nine Steps*. In *Mr Standfast* both types of Scotland, the city and country, are pitched against each other, and both are suppressed. Striking workers who endanger their country must be watched closely, and Highlanders must be cleared, as Hannay regretfully decides as he accepts hospitality from an elderly Highland couple on Skye. These things are sad but they must be so for the imperial project. Increasingly, the portrait of the rural in irreversible decline and the urban in all consuming growth carried over into Scottish books and films, even those where only one of those versions appears. The rural was the remembered, the longed-for; the urban was the hated, the here and now, the real. The rural was magical; the urban was pitiless. The rural was Romantic, a term often conflated with 'Kailyard'; the urban was gritty and grim. The rural was soft, its hills and skies and flowing rivers shot in dissolving focus. The urban, assisted in this image by many films, crime books, thrillers and some mainstream literary work, was hard – stones, black tenement, chimneys, filthy water gurgling in gutters, its storylines filled with rising tension, deadpan street talk and abrupt dramatic peaks tricked out in expressionist realism, as in McIlvanney's *Laidlaw*:

> Glasgow was home-made ginger biscuits and Jennifer Lawson dead in the park. It was the sententious niceness of the Commander and the threatened abrasiveness of Laidlaw. It was Milligan, insensitive as a mobile slab of cement, and Mrs Lawson, witless with hurt. It was the right hand knocking you down and the left hand picking you up, while the mouth alternated apology and threat.

Seen by most artists as either in permanent decline or a myth in the first place, the Romantic version faded through the 20th century. But both it and the hellish city still exist and continue to be used as deliberate contrasts even in recent fiction, as in Iain Banks's *Complicity* where the urban is the cramped, addicted high of cars, drugs and video games, and the rural (for the most part) is the remembered place of friendship, fun, physical exertion and well-being. The Scottish rural landscape and Scottish cities have changed beyond recognition in the last 30 years, and they're still changing, but this opposition persists in our fiction, particularly its screen versions. The false binary of these two Scotlands – false because they're only two among many – still dominates our viewing.

There is however a third place in Scottish literature, somewhere that lies outside the duality of city and country without disturbing it, and that is the place of exile. Hundreds of thousands of Scots emigrated to the colonies to establish communities which preserved language, culture and tradition sometimes better than was done at home. In Scottish fiction the exiled Scot simply disappears. Exile is an unknown place where essential Scottishness (a mystical set of qualities which have never been defined) is changed or lost or diluted in some way so that return is never possible. The returned Scot is no longer a true Scot, altered by having left his native land generations before or when he was younger, his essential identity watered down or changed so that he can be neither an example to the rest of us nor any kind of solution. This truly miserablist stance, fundamentally linked to predestination (those who escape our fate can no longer be of us), can apply anywhere in Scotland, Highland or Lowland, urban or rural, rich or poor. Another way of putting it is Christopher Harvie's version, where exile makes different kinds of Scots, the 'red' ones who left and took part in Empire and the 'black' ones (presumably the grimmer variety) who stayed behind and resisted it. Even when the exile attempts it, his return isn't possible. In *Home* by Iain Crichton Smith the ex-Scot Jamieson, now South African, no longer knows where home is, who he is or where on earth he came from. The dirty tenement block he visits, where he and his wife spent the early years of their marriage, is exactly the same as when they left and also utterly changed, a brutal collision of the ada-mantine and the debased, like Jamieson himself:

> And the wallet bulged from his breast pocket. A wife, two children, and a good job in administration.

He finds a sense of belonging only when he steps into his hotel, and even there it is scattered between the red-faced 'men who ran Scotland' drinking in the bar, memories – not of Scotland – but of Africa, and agonisingly vivid impressions of possessions.

> He sniffed his whisky, swirling it around in the glass, golden and clear and thin and burningly pure.

Exile is different from the place McLethie and John Grey slink to after their defeat in *No Mean City*, which is the hell of shame. Nor is it the place Harry Gibbon comes across on his European adventure, or where Rona and Cassie drive though in Janice Galloway's *Foreign Parts*, or the Dutch housing scheme inhabited by the narrator of 'Eurotrash'. These travelling Scots remain Scots because return is allowed to them, and is in fact inevitable. They take a strong feeling of being disoriented with them on their travels, the knowledge that they're in the wrong place and the strong suspicion that it's all nonsense – they'll never escape what they're fleeing or find what they're looking for anyway. Miserablism is in their mental baggage. They see their original predicament in everything around them even as they try to 'move on'. But exile is different from these possibilities. It's the loss of the people who experience it, forever. Their history since they left can't count – the traditions they've continued or started in the meantime can't be brought back or re-incorporated. Nothing about them can be real – which is to say, Scottish – because they've escaped the thing that is the true test, the stuck state of miserablism. By dodging fate they cease to exist. The mental geography of Scottish miserablism permits no alternatives.

Romanticism eventually became an empty, boastful tale, a bravemouth assertion of 'wha's like us?' mixed up with a meaningless jumble of symbols – flags, kilts, lions rampant and thistles. Coupled with the delusion that the Scots invented everything (penicillin, whisky, football, the television, the telephone) and the startling assertion that Scots aren't bigoted (English people who live in Scotland would probably beg to differ), it was a tale that had wandered so far from reality that it needed scoured, taken back to its basics. Murray Grigor's *Scotch Myths* exhibition in 1979 did just that, deconstructing the myth so thoroughly that it seemed as if Romantic kitsch might disappear forever. *Scotch Myths* was a piece of political art which led in turn to the *Cinema in a Small Nation* conference and from there to the *Scotch Reels* collection of essays in 1982. *Scotch Reels* is probably the most influential book ever written about Scottish cinema and kick-started it as a subject worthy of serious study and criticism. It is also the most controversial book there is on the subject and thoroughly miserablist from start to finish. It offers one or two hints about where film might go but it is much more concerned with what's wrong, which is everything, sorting it into categories so as to blast them with Calvinist zeal. The Tartanry of Walt Disney's *Bonnie Prince Charlie*, the Clydesidism of *To Sea the Great Ships*, the Kailyardism of *The Little Minister* – all are smitten by the Scotch Reels contributors' wrath. The point, as ever in miserablism – in this case a collection of critical essays and an exhibition – is not to suggest ways out of the situation but to criticise what's there at the moment and show us why the trap can't be broken. So scathing was *Scotch Reels* in its condemnation that it excluded the only two filmmakers who were actually making new Scottish films at the time, Bill Douglas (perhaps the supreme miserablist in Scottish film) and Bill Forsyth, in many ways his opposite.

The political model of Scottish miserablism was a powerful one. Produced in one field by the *Scotch Reels* contributors and by writers like James Kelman in another, it was hugely perceptive of Scottish society in the last third of the 20th century. It was made all the more influential by the fact that Kelman introduced a new subtlety and intellectualism to the basic model. It identified the fixed, subservient role of many Scots inside their own culture and the ways in which that culture failed to represent the reality of their lives. By engaging directly and fiercely with Scottish art it helped put Scotland on the map as a place that actually cared about, and was prepared to fight for, the way it was depicted. It began an upsurge of interest in Scottish culture which encouraged the return of many who had left to work elsewhere in theatre, film and television and, with increasing international interest in the work of Kelman, Alasdair Gray and others of their circle, helped build what nobody had really expected, a surge of optimism. This brought with it in turn, in the wake of the Garden Festival in 1988 and the City of Culture in 1990, an influx of talented, interested, curious and ambitious newcomers, sometimes the sons and daughters of Scottish expatriates keen to return to their spiritual home and join the vibrant artistic scene that was swiftly emerging in Scottish art, cinema and television. It's sad that we sometimes turn on these people with accusations of 'incomers' and 'white settlers'. But it's very Scottish and very miserablist to judge everything by its fault-lines. And we should remember that miserablism can't offer solutions, only the dismal facts. Like any dominant mode, which Kelmanesque miserablism was at the time, the prevailing image of the real city with its portraits of pub-based, inarticulate, expletive-exploding yet existential men spawned many less worthy imitators who went on reproducing the more trite parts of the message as it passed from the radical to the merely fashionable and then became a parody of itself, as in the later work of Irvine Welsh. (Indeed, Welsh's own fate as an artist, condemned forever to repeat the same book again and again, making it a little bit worse each time, and then to turn it into increasingly bad films, is a truly miserablist one.)

Women writers in particular struggled to escape the miserablist mindset that focused for the greatest part on men's experiences. It was accompanied by the fact, borne out in broadcasting statistics, that virtually all Scottish screenwriting, directing and producing was by men. Women's experiences, imagination and writing seemed permanently destined for the ghetto, a dusty shelf in the library or the video store labelled 'women's', or hidden away at the back of a bookshop if a woman writer was lucky enough to be published at all. This was to change, but not necessarily to the satisfaction of those who felt that the best writing time of their lives had been wasted by a lack of publishing opportunities. It is a fact that in much Scottish art, but particularly in film and television where the commissioning process encourages timidity and sameness, the miserablist male still dominates.

New prose and poetry can explore different topics and subjects because little depends on it other than a modest publishing budget (or increasingly in these digital days, no budget at all) and the writer's self-esteem. But film and television demand investment, salaries and profit. Screen drama is much more conservative, much less flexible and much more susceptible to the continuance of dominant modes long after the time has come for their quiet withdrawal. And these safe, tried-and-tested stereotypes (the snarling male, the sublime hills, the gritty city and so on) are, of course, defended by the actors, writers and producers who've made their names and dubious reputations by doing nothing more than rehash the same old story. It's the way these factors have reinforced the image of dominant masculinity in the film and television industries over the last 25 or so years, propping it up as it lost its potency and its meaning as its social context and its roots changed, that we'll examine in the subsequent chapters.

In books, there is now a huge amount of variety. It's possible today to write about a Jewish salesman in the Highlands (J David Simons, *The Credit Draper*), a young girl during the Clydebank blitz (Sue Reid Sexton, *Mavis's Shoe*), a woman's real-life quest for her grandmother's lost child (Eleanor Thom, *Crosshouse*), a search for a missing Thai bride (Andrea McNicoll, *Narratives from No Man's Land*), a young academic's search for a poet's lost legacy (Louise Welsh, *Naming the Bones*), a South African's search for her real 'black' identity (Zoe Wicomb, *Playing in the Light*) or two women's attempts to preserve their way of life on a remote island (Margaret Elphinstone, *Light*). All of these are new or recent novels based in or written from Scotland. They cross boundaries of gender, class, geography, genre and time without restriction. They have resourceful women, sensitive men, immigrants, children, historical characters and even people with English accents for their protagonists. They move from the city to the country and from Scotland to other parts of the world with ease. They use crime, love, murder, memoir, comedy, horror, fantasy, creative non-fiction, and realism as the means of making their stories. They don't necessarily fall within the boundaries of genre although there are many well-written, interesting new books that use their genre with knowledge and respect (Gordon Brown, *Falling*; Douglas Thompson, *Ultrameta*; Michael J. Malone, *Blood Tears*). Scottish writing today is black, white, Asian, Polish, disabled, polemic, quiet, criminal, urban or rural and often both.

Children's fiction, graphic novels, comics, films, television and online forms, writing that is entirely digital or partly digital and partly print in new variations like crowd-funded means of production, are all valid parts of it, and often where its most interesting aspects are to be found.

What's more, in-depth study of the writing of any era shows that this diversity in prose and poetry, far from being particular to our age, has always been the case, although there have been high and low points in its quality. Scott and Hogg and their contemporaries wrote an enormous amount of material – fantasy, gothic tales, the supernatural, historical romances, early forms of science fiction and many other kinds of story, including dark and realistic ones. The macabre, the exaggerated, the ludicrous and the real could also be mixed together into fantastic new concoctions, as in the *Noctes Ambrosianae*, the comic collaborative series produced in *Blackwood's* from 1825. Scott, abandoning the epic poem, invented the historical novel in *Waverley* (1814). In *Rob Roy* (1817) he found a way to show the Highlands' and Lowlands' close relationship to each other while also acknowledging their difference (Bailie Nicol Jarvie, the representative of Lowland commercialism, and Rob Roy, the wild noble Highlander, are brothers-in-law, not strangers to each other and not incompatible). Far from being 'mere' historical romances, Scott's novels were mixtures of fiction, history, Romanticism, antiquarianism, contemporary politics and his own imagination. Meanwhile Hogg and his contemporaries like John Gibson Lockhart, Walter Maginn, John Wilson, Thomas de Quincey, Robert Sym, James Grey and David Moir and some female writers such as Mary Brunton and Susan Ferrier, all of them writing in Scott's shadow, hacked out a vast variety of articles, tales, ballads, songs, novels, journalism and reviews for journals like *Blackwood's*, *The Scots Magazine* and *Fraser's*. There were dark tales and many gothic versions of them. The tortured hero was one striking character of the period (as in *Extracts from Gosschen's Diary No. 1*, attributed to John Wilson), but there were a thousand others. He was only one of many archetypes that inhabited fiction.

Perhaps the miserablist hero is set to last longest in crime fiction, still popular and widely-read as large publishing houses collapse under the strain of digital competition and their own inability to face the future. Maybe he'll continue to investigate things, suffering a permanent hangover/divorce/anxiety as he stalks the grim streets, although there are signs that even his days are numbered as crime fiction becomes bolder, more intelligent and more willing to move away from its self-imposed limitations, as female investigators, queer detectives or even literary figures take up his role. Or maybe he's finally reached his end in the figure of the serial killer running for his life, sickened by his power and longing for his end. The supposed inability of crime fiction and the thriller to handle politics, social comment and philosophy – never a valid claim in the first place – may be changing at last as these forms begin to reconsider themselves and become more complex and less concerned with easy contrasts, with the black and white, the fatally divided, the predestined.

It's the miserablist's fate always to find fault elsewhere, because he is indeed not to blame. But when the potency of that original message has been lost, when it's all society's/the drink's/the English's fault, it's time to move on. In the forthcoming referendum many will vote for independence because they believe it's time Scotland takes responsibility for itself. But whatever the result of that ballot, miserablists will have to change. They can't sustain their permanent adolescence forever. And we as writers and artists may have to abandon our cherished affection for only the extremes, for fixed duality, and understand that truths also lie with everything in between.

In the light of the fluid and dynamic response of new Scottish writing to change and the ever-shifting nature of the Scottish political and cultural landscape, it is disgraceful, and absurd, that today's commissioners for broadcast and film production still turn to the usual stories, the miserablist narratives, dinosaurs treading the path towards their own extinction – the half-baked gangsters, the enraged alcoholics, the murderer in the crime story that doesn't care about the victim, the Hard Man whose Hardness repeats itself in endless drug deals and kidnappings, the skulking shirker, the tenement dirker, the snarling cop, the menacing boss, monstrous males endlessly reverting to their natural Calibans. Their function has long disappeared and was only ever a bad copy of something good in the first place. The dearth of high quality new Scottish broadcast drama points not to a paucity of original material but to a paucity of ideas among screen practitioners and commissioners and those who make a living from portraying us on the screen – and also to their complete lack of awareness of the explosion of creativity that is happening now on the ground in

Scotland. Everyone in Scotland is a writer now, or at least that is how it sometimes seems to appear in certain quarters. Our greatest export is the diversity of our fiction, the myriad of alternatives between its contrasts and all its new heroes and heroines. It's time we knew it.

CHAPTER THREE

To See Ourselves As Others See Us

ELEANOR YULE

THE MAJORITY OF film theorists agree that depictions of Scotland have polarised around two opposite expressions, the Kailyard and the anti-Kailyard, or for the purposes of this argument, the Kailyard and Scottish miserablism. For film theorist Jane Sillars the Kailyard is the cabbage patch that is the antithesis of miserablism. It chooses rural settings in which to tell 'sentimentalised tales of small town life'.

In her essay *Admitting the Kailyard*, Sillars describes the tension created by these 'opposing conceptions of Scotland as:

> a cultural battle that rages across the 20th century between the confines of the Kailyard and the ejaculatory range of anti-Kailyard... the conflict between a desire to belong and the desperation to escape; between an idealised Scotland and one left trampled in the dust; between identity seen as rooted and safe or seen as stale and stagnant; between closed and opened Scotlands.

The figures of Jekyll and Hyde can be seen as two conflicting representations of Scottishness that show the nation as a 'divided self', a fractured psyche which thrives in reaction to its alienated other half. It could be argued that both the Kailyard (used in this sense to mean the images also created and distributed by Romanticism) and miserablism, within film, are by their very nature anachronistic depictions. One conjures up a rural idyll shattered by the Clearances and the rise of heavy industry, the other wallows in the after effects of post-industrial collapse in Scotland's cities, in reality an evolving landscape of redevelopment since the '60s.

And of course, much of this desire to depict rural Scotland as a place of nostalgia comes from the yearning created by mass exile and from the large displaced diaspora separated, by the likes of the *Queen Mary* liner, from the rolling glens and misty mountains of home.

Kailyard cinema has tended to mythologise the Scottish Highlands and sentimentalise Celtic culture. It has also, more often than not, been created by outsiders, many with roots in Scotland, for the consumption of other outsiders and exiles, catering predominantly for an expatriate Scots sensibility. Miserablism, on the other hand, once showed a version of Scotland insiders didn't want outsiders to see, but like Kailyard it has now become an exportable national commodity, projecting an image of Scotland that outsiders *do* see and believe to be 'real'.

But like miserablism, Kailyard blends a particular fantasy of Scotland with authentic cultural observations. Critical mistrust towards the Kailyard can be traced to a historical tendency to invent bogus legends and legacies which reinvented Scotland as a heroic and mythical place. Colin McArthur, the editor of the controversial *Scotch Reels* collection, traces this tradition in Scottish culture:

> The Scottish Discursive unconscious has been constructed over several centuries, its key architects including James 'Ossian' MacPherson, Sir Walter Scott, Felix Mendelssohn, Queen Victoria, Sir Edward Landseer and Sir Harry Lauder. Within it a dream Scotland emerges which is highland, wild, 'feminine', close to nature and which has, above all, the capacity to enchant and transform the stranger.

Powell and Pressburger's *I Know Where I'm Going* (1945), Alexander Mackendrick's *Whisky Galore!* (1949) and Vincente Minnelli's Hollywood musical *Brigadoon* (1954), all represent rural Scotland as a cosy, recreational wilderness populated by small supportive communities ready to welcome visitors. They also share a mood of post-war optimism, meaning these films celebrate rather than deconstruct (as in miserablism) the idea of a functioning and generous Scottish community.

These Kailyard visions of misty glens and tartan-clad folk may be rose-tinted but many of the positive values they celebrate do exist within Scottish cultural history. All three of the above films are united in their depiction of the Scots as warm, welcoming and above all hospitable. 'Hospitality is a virtue of which my countrymen may be proud of the reputation', writes a minister from Shetland in the early 19th century.

> In the majority of cases the favour lies most truly not on the side of the guest, but on that of the host; and in a country where inns can

hardly be said to exist, kindness to strangers becomes a sacred duty, which no temporary inconvenience can cancel.

MARTIN

In *I Know Where I'm Going* (1945), Joan Webster (Wendy Hiller), a feisty, ambitious Londoner travels to the west coast of Scotland hoping to get to the Island of Kiloran owned by her rich industrial boss, who she plans to marry there. However, she is prevented by the Scottish weather, forcing her to seek hospitality on the mainland from the local residents while she waits for the storms to clear. Exposure to the locals and their rural and free way of life forces Joan to get in touch with her own true authentic nature and see through the hollow self-seeking values of industry and materialism. Most significantly space is given within the film not just to feminine qualities of landscape and culture but to the feisty female protagonist, Joan, who drives the narrative.

After being drowned (almost literally at one point in the Corryvreckan whirlpool) by hospitality, Joan falls for local chap Torquil MacNeil, the impoverished and rightful Laird of Kiloran, an island now owned by her rich fiancé whom she rejects. The film's message is clear. In Michael Powell's words, 'kindness rules the world, not money'.

Scottish rural culture is depicted as healing, instinctive and beautiful and, as Colin McArthur mentions, feminine – unlike the bleak testosterone-driven world of miserablism.

Both outsiders to Scottish culture, Kent-born Michael Powell and Hungarian Jew Emeric Pressburger co-wrote the screenplay of *I Know Where I'm Going* in the closing year of the Second World War. Michael Powell states in his biography that by then Britain had been 'at war for so long, that we are beginning to forget fundamental truths. It is time they were reinstated'. On the verge of a new age, which would see Clement Attlee's government implement the welfare state in Britain, Powell and Pressburger searched for a location to set their story where the 'authentic' values that they wanted to 'reinstate' were still intact. The Western Highlands was a convincing choice. As outsiders they had the distance to see this clearly, as well as regarding the Highland scenery and Gaelic language as rich and exotic. Powell talks about the process of writing:

According to our usual plan of work, my job was to add and to change the location sequences, bringing in all I had learnt of the authentic dialogue, atmosphere and names of the Western Isles. I ransacked Monty McKenzie's pot-boiling novels for Gaelic phrases and idioms.

Kailyard films also thrive on what Cairns Craig describes as 'the myths by which Scotland conceals itself', something the late auteur and father of miserablism Bill Douglas deconstructs in his powerful autobiographical *Childhood Trilogy* (1972–8). Within the Kailyard, however, myth is celebrated rather than exploded, and used to both escape and re-imagine the grim landscape of the miserablist.

Pressburger cites Sir Walter Scott as one of his influences when writing the screenplay of *I Know Where I'm Going*, particularly in the addition of a family curse to the plot. Pressburger believed that as much as his audience would 'expect' to see pastoral mountains and glens they would also 'expect' a curse, another part of the Scottish mythical landscape.

However in Kailyard texts, curses are rarely stronger than the protagonist. *I Know Where I'm Going* demonstrates that authentic values will always win out, that kindness will win over materiality. In miserablism the opposite takes place. Goodness will always be defeated, squashed down or suppressed, while familial curses thrive for generations.

The curse in *I Know Where I'm Going* turns out to be a delightful double entendre that unites, rather than separates, the protagonists in love. 'Never shall he leave this castle a free man' reads the epithet written in stone on the castle walls. By kissing Joan in the castle grounds Torquil has activated the curse against his ancestors. He has risked everything for love. But there's a twist. 'He shall be chained to a woman until the end of his days and he shall die in his chains'. In the Kailyard context, the curse is a blessing in disguise. Joan and Torquil will be united not as enemies but as man and wife, making the vengeful curse impotent, turning imprisonment into partnership and proving what Powell and Pressburger set out to show, that 'there is nothing stronger than love'.

Emeric Pressburger's contribution to Scottish culture did not end with this film. His grandsons, film producer Andrew and Oscar-winning director Kevin MacDonald, were both raised in Scotland and have made important contributions to both the Scottish and British film industries, including a key miserablist text, *Trainspotting*, which Andrew MacDonald produced five decades after his grandfather wrote *I Know Where I'm Going*, a Kailyard classic.

American director's Vincent Minnelli's Technicolor extravaganza, *Brigadoon*, has much in common with Powell and Pressburger's film. In *Brigadoon*, the Highland community is also depicted as beautiful, loving, and above all effective, something outsiders envy and don't want to leave behind.

Brigadoon is a mythical village where the old Highland traditions have been successfully preserved, left untainted by the industrial age or the ravages of the then recent world wars. Brigadoon village only appears to the outside world once a century, keeping it safe from outside corruption and making it tantalisingly difficult for outsiders to penetrate. Like Bill Forsyth's *Local Hero* (1982) the protagonists, always outsiders, discover inside these Scottish communities the 'heart' that is missing in their own materialistic culture.

When the tartan draped citizens of *Brigadoon* burst into song for New York interloper Tommy Albright (Gene Kelly), they sing about personal sacrifice and monogamy. Within the Kailyard, relationships between men and women are generally respectful, loving and peaceable, unlike miserablism where they break down in conflict and disappointment. In *Go Home with Bonnie Jean*, Charlie sings about what he has given up for Jean. He tells us, 'I used to be a rovin' lad, a rovin' and wandering life I had', then one day he saw a 'maid' and he tells us his 'tavern days are over' and now he, 'goes home with Bonnie Jean'.

The message within this Kailyard classic is that it is possible to grow up, mature, have meaningful committed relationships *and* be Scottish. Charlie gives up drinking to excess for the love of his lassie. In miserablism, the hero can't overcome his addictions or grow up so he continues to 'wander' in all senses of the word – he fraternises with low company in the taverns and he fails to go home with his bonnie wife, who instead anxiously waits for him alone with the weans.

Whisky Galore! (1949) further explores the Scots love affair with alcohol. Here it does not wreck communities but unites them, inspiring them to work together towards a common purpose. In *Whisky Galore!* the islanders of Todday are in crisis – they have run out of whisky, so when a ship carrying 50,000 cases happens to run aground nearby, the community pull together to outwit the stuffy English commander Captain Waggett (Basil Radford), whose job it is to safeguard the booty. The islanders use their wit, cunning and strategy as tools to successfully smuggle the whisky and replenish their supplies. Captain Waggett, a pompous, authoritarian outsider, and George Campbell's domineering, staunchly Calvinist mother, an islander herself, are both seen as fair game and outsmarted by locals. After all the locals are only reclaiming what's already culturally theirs. Whisky. In another scenario it could be oil. Land. Wind. Water.

Whisky Galore! depicts the Scots as a successful race, not as victims who are, according to *Trainspotting's* Renton 'colonised by wankers' or 'ruled by effete arseholes' but as rather intelligent folk who, by drawing on each other's strengths, can re-possess their own cultural legacy.

The director of *Whisky Galore!*, Alexander Mackendrick, claims to have had an American perspective but a Scottish soul, and felt his Scottishness acutely. He claimed 'nationality is a very curious thing. The blood is Scots and the temperament is Scots but I am in fact 100 per cent American'. Although from Scottish stock Mackendrick was born and bred in Boston only arriving in Scotland to study at the Glasgow School of Art, before famously going on to work for the Ealing Studios, directing some of their most successful output including *Man in a White Suit* (1951) and *The Ladykillers* (1955).

Mackendrick's time at Ealing taught him many things, but the collaborative nature of the work ethos within the studio system also gave him a unique insight into how effective communities can be structured, particularly on the film set. Martin Scorsese explains in his foreword to Mackendrick's *On Film Making*:

> For Mackendrick, the very word 'director' implied being in control of other people's skill just as much, if not more, than the exercise of one's own craftsmanship. As he explained, 'the true role of a director involves more than having practical experience in various technical skills – it means functioning as a leader who is able to give directions to a group of other talented individuals'. In fact the great directors, he suggested, 'dissolve and disappear into the work' while making other people look good... 'the director is merely a channel for other people's talents'.

Mackendrick railed against the tyranny of the 'auteur', believing that power and control were inhibiting factors within a creative environment, resulting in hierarchies and division. In *The Spirit Level* (2009) Richard Wilkinson and Kate Pickett argue that the creation of inequality within society produces devastatingly negative effects on the self-esteem of its citizens. Miserablism with its underdog hero and dysfunctional communities reflects the damage of this late capitalistic tendency to divide and rule at all costs. Kailyard, on the other hand, offers a different vision, one that empowers and often creates alternatives, even if they are hard to implement in reality.

Mackendrick's depiction of an indigenous but united Scottish community shows each citizen being respected for who and what they are. All are entitled to their fair share of the treasure. This ethos of equality was not restricted to Mackendrick's fiction, he also directly applied it to the working conditions on the film sets he ran, ensuring that each member of a film crew was appreciated, respected and free to contribute towards a stronger more creative whole. The fact that the films he created at the Ealing Studios were among their most successful is testimony to the way he went about this collaborative way of working.

Box office success *Braveheart* (1995) was less of a collaboration and more of a vehicle for its Oscar-winning director and lead US/Australian actor Mel Gibson to explore the legendary 13th-century Scots rebel Sir William Wallace. Gibson, himself of Irish extraction, worked closely with screenwriter Randall Wallace, who in common with other Kailyard creators was drawn to Wallace's story through what he felt was his own genetic connection. 'Before I wrote the film', claimed Wallace,

> I had never heard of William Wallace and his story seemed so romantic to me. I think he is an ancestor, I feel his blood in my veins. I can't prove it but then no one can disprove it.

As well as winning five Oscars and grossing nearly 300 million dollars, the film also became synonymous with the campaign for Scottish devolution and according to Gibson influenced the outcome of the 1997 referendum and the establishment of a Scottish parliament at Holyrood.

> I became really aware of what a piece of art could do to change things... Scotland had received partial autonomy, but I think the film

started the ball rolling on some stuff… On the way to the premiere in Scotland the crowd was 50-deep and I couldn't believe there was so much feeling and fervour about the subject. It hit a chord, definitely.

The tribal image of Wallace (Gibson) astride his warhorse, face smeared in blue paint, appealing to his fellow villagers to join him in battle against Edward, Hammer of the Scots, has become a symbol of nationalistic fervor. It is also, like *Whisky Galore!,* a fictionalised example of what the Scots are capable of if they unite, become effective and start to take responsibility for their own destiny. Wallace's now famous monologue from *Braveheart* speaks for itself:

> I am William Wallace. And I see a whole army of my countrymen, here in defiance of tyranny! You have come to fight as free men. And free man you are!… And dying in your bed many years from now, would you be willing to trade all the days from this day to that, for one chance, just one chance, to come back here as young men and tell our enemies that they may take our lives but they will never take our freedom!

In his 2007 book *Affluenza*, Oliver James presents evidence that our quest for material happiness and riches within Western society is creating the opposite result, causing mass depression, anxiety and an increase in addiction. Contrary to our capitalistic programming, James argues, money, power and wealth cannot, and are not, making us happy. Through his research James discovered other values that he proves matter more to human contentment than materialistic gain. Those values – 'authenticity', 'effectivity' and 'community' – are all present in the films examined above. They may show idealised versions of Scotland but they offer a vision of a nation where those values are not only ingrained within the culture but are the envy of outsiders, something the Scots find very hard to see for themselves.

An outsider who has, more recently, contributed to Scottish film and TV output is American-born writer and director Annie Griffin. Griffin explored contemporary Scottish culture in her award-winning TV comedy series, *The Book Group* (2002–3), produced by her Glasgow-based company Pirate Productions for Channel Four. In an interview for the *Scotsman* in 2009, Griffin revealed her disappointment at the lack of Scottish-based fiction on the British television networks and the sharp decline in its output from the '90s.

> There is an appetite around Britain to see things set in Scotland... We are starved of it. I think it is outrageous that we don't have more Scottish drama on our screens.

Griffin's 'outsider' status has allowed her free rein to re-imagine a diverse community within a Scottish post-millennial context, something she believes is missing from indigenous TV output.

> What is strange is this Scottish mentality that television from Scotland is low-brow... There's a worry that things can be 'too Scottish'. That's not something I'm burdened with. I love Scotland, especially the glory and the sinister sides of Edinburgh, but though the country has out-performed in the other arts – music, literature and such – it doesn't in broadcasting. That's a terrible shame.

The Book Group features characters rarely given an outing in Scottish film and TV fiction. As well as a strong idiosyncratic American female protagonist, Clare Pettengill (Anne Dudek), newly arrived in Glasgow, Griffin's male characters are paradoxical and unique, subverting the working class archetypes of the miserablist text. Posh student Lachlan Glendinning (James Lance) is a drug addict, football supporter Rab (Derek Riddel) is a closet bisexual while lifeguard Kenny McLeod (Rory McCann) is wheel-chair-bound. What Griffin does with *The Book Group*, her BAFTA winning feature film debut, *Festival* (2005), set during the Edinburgh Fringe, and more recently in her TV comedy pilot, *New Town* (2009), is explore middle- and upper-class Scottish culture. She does this through comedic characters, many of them incomers to Scotland's Central Belt, using locations that have dominated as Scottish settings not just within miserbalism, but in the majority of mainstream Scottish TV drama as well.

After her success with *Festival* in 2005, Griffin pitched *New Town* (2009), a drama-comedy series to the BBC network in London. Griffin's approach was refreshingly original within a Scottish context, but it also caught the spirit of the ongoing property crisis.

> I was really interested in the anxiety that people have around housing which I think has become worse since the credit crunch. Housing,

especially in this country, seems to call up people's most anxious desires and you can never get it right. Trying to have your perfect living space is traumatic.

Unlike the majority of ideas from writers based in Scotland about Scotland, *New Town* was fortunate enough to pass the scrutiny of the BBC Controllers in London. Unusually, the scripts for the entire six part series were commissioned for development and a sizeable chunk of money was paid out to Griffin from the public purse. Much like *The Book Group*, Griffin wanted to bring a culturally eclectic mix of characters to the screen, framed within a Scottish world, in this case the cosmopolitan, elite and often cut-throat world of Edinburgh's New Town. For the pilot episode, which Griffin directed, she chose a strong cast who had appealed to a national audience. Scottish actress Daniella Nardini played Meredith McIlvanney, a stylish, ruthless estate agent while *The League of Gentlemen*'s Mark Gatiss was cast as a gay architect with Obsessive Compulsive Disorder.

In February 2009 the *New Town* pilot was eventually broadcast after a six-month delay. Despite being initially well received by its BBC commissioners and TV reviewers the series was inexplicably cancelled. The five completed scripts Griffin had been commissioned to write remain unproduced.

Since 2009, Griffin, like many other innovative and talented Scottish writers and directors, has been absorbed into the Manchester-based Scottish diaspora. Unable, at the time, to find either an outlet for her own work or suitable employment in Scotland due to a lack of drama production there, Griffin went south to Salford to find work, like many other up-and-coming Scottish film and television writers and producers, where she was hired to direct Channel Four's freshers' drama *Fresh Meat* (2011–12), written by *Peep Show* team Jesse Armstrong and Sam Bain, which was shot and set in Manchester's Medlock University.

The sharp decline in network drama output from Scotland from both the BBC and STV, which brought *Taggart* to a close in 2011, decreased still further the amount of work for Scottish-based talent. In the opening months of 2009 the Association of Film and TV Practitioners Scotland (AFTPS) was created. Their Facebook page stated that the group was 'set up by people working in the film and television industry in Scotland as a political lobbying group to counter the growing levels of unemployment and lack of prospects in Scotland.' By raising awareness they aim to 'increase Scottish-based commissioning' and to create 'greater support for indigenous Scottish-based production companies'.

Of the 270 professionals who joined the AFTPS when it formed in 2009, 40 per cent claimed they had had less than 20 days work that year. BBC Scotland responded by claiming that the creation and production of a derivative soap, *River City* along with other initiatives, would help create a healthy and sustainable industry. Another solution, brainchild of the divisive BBC's Nations and Regions Policy, was to relocate the highly popular school drama series *Waterloo Road* (2006–13) from Rochdale to Greenock, hoping to reverse the Scottish flow of talent from Glasgow. The BBC commissioned 50 hour-long episodes over the next two years, and the independent company responsible for production, Shed Productions, estimated that the series would generate £25 million in direct investment as well as creating 230 jobs. Expat Scot Eileen Gallagher, Scottish chief executive of Shed, told reporters it would help Scotland 'grow' more TV drama.

> If you think about it, Manchester has *Coronation Street*, Yorkshire has *Emmerdale*, London has *EastEnders* and Cardiff has *Casualty* now and what does Glasgow have? It now has *Waterloo Road*.
>
> MILLER

However, neither of these strategies tackled the basic problem outlined by the AFTPS, for which they continue to lobby, which is the urgent need for increasing Scottish-based commissioning of indigenous stories and original ideas. Editorial control for the majority of Scottish TV drama output still remains in London. The networks defend the lack of the commissioning of indigenously created content in Scotland by claiming that the ideas they receive from writers and independent companies based in Scotland are weaker than their other network competitors, which seems directly at odds with Scotland's global reputation for new prose fiction and the high percentage of award-winning Scottish radio plays by Scottish-based writers on Radio Four.

The question must be asked: what is it the TV networks are actually looking for from Scotland? Again, using Griffin's *New Town* as an example, the evidence points to commissioning only ideas that originated in London or the two staples of Scottish fiction, miserablism and the Kailyard.

The networks' taste for old-fashioned Scottish Kailyard comedy was manifested most recently in *Bob Servant* (starring Brian Cox), an adaptation of the successful Radio Four series. Although written by Scottish-based writer Neil Forsyth, and refreshingly located in Dundee, it has been described by critics as 'utterly plodding... desperately old fashioned' (Rachel Cooke, *New Statesman*) and in the *Daily Telegraph* as 'not funny, despite the best efforts of Cox in the title role'.

Nevertheless, over the decades, a few projects have managed to sneak past the polarised tastes of network commissioners. Indigenous Scottish creators have managed to secure a few intermittent commissions, particularly in the area of TV comedy, that tiptoe a path between the kitsch sentimentality of the Kailyard and the hardcore social realism of miserablism. Despite their artistic excellence and/or popularity, examples either tend to be one-off commissions or series that don't return.

Among them are *Tutti Frutti* (1987), *Your Cheatin' Heart* (1990) and *Boswell and Johnson's Tour of the Western Isles* (1993) all from the pen of writer and director John Byrne, whose work has been conspicuously absent from British television since the mid-'90s, a time when miserablism was entrenching itself as a national brand among the London commissioners. Similarly Forbes Masson's and Alan Cummings' camp airline spoof *The High Life* (1994–5), now heralded as a cult classic, was not re-commissioned after the first series, a safer bet at that time being the popular and well-established *Rab C Nesbitt,* which ran for 20 years satisfying English preconceptions of Scottish working-class culture.

Hardeep Singh Kohli's Scottish Asian comedy for the Channel Four network, *Meet the Magoons* (2002) suffered a similar fate. Despite receiving plaudits from hard-nosed *Sunday Times* critic A A Gill, who believed the show 'might well evolve into something classic', a second series was never commissioned.

Many of these original Scottish comedies owe an unconscious debt to filmmaker Bill Forsyth who introduced a gentle lyricism into the Scottish oeuvre. Forsyth was almost unique in his ability to synergise the post-war optimism of Mackendrick's Ealing comedies with the 'reality' of Scottish contemporary culture. Forsyth's idiosyncratic humour, apparent in films such as *That Sinking Feeling* (1979), *Comfort and Joy* (1984) *and Local Hero* (1983) also connected to audiences internationally, although ironically Forsyth's breakthrough film *Gregory's Girl* (1981) had to be re-voiced for the American market due to the unknown cast's 'strong' Scottish accents.

Determined to go ahead with production for *Gregory's Girl*, Forsyth originally planned to shoot it on 16mm film for a meagre £29,000, but ended up attracting £200,000. It was shot on 35mm and therefore showable on cinema screens. In contrast, a British film made in the same year, the multi-Oscar-winning *Chariots of Fire* (1981), had a budget of £3 million, over 15 times that of its Scottish counterpart. On its release *Gregory's Girl* was an unexpected and enormous success, particularly in America, taking a staggering 25 million, 125 times its original budget compared to the more widely distributed *Chariots* which took only 16 times its budget.

It is interesting to note that *Chariots of Fire* was not only partially shot in Scotland (the Old Course and beach in St Andrews) but also had a Scottish central character, real life missionary and Olympic champion Eric Liddell (Ian Charleston). The Lancastrian screenwriter Colin Welland, who won an Oscar for Best Original Screenplay was one of the early influences on Scottish screenwriter Peter McDougall, who was beginning to write some of the hardest hitting and most powerful works of the miserablist canon. Yet *Chariots* was marketed as a British 'Heritage' movie, tapping into notions of Empire and fueling a resurgence of British nationalism, encouraged by Margaret Thatcher's government and the extensive hype surrounding the Royal Wedding in 1981. Colin Welland is famous for declaring 'the British are coming' after *Chariots* won an impressive seven academy awards at the Oscars. He was referring to the British film industry but it was a phrase that could equally apply to the Falklands War which broke out the following year.

Bill Forsyth's focus was entirely different, as was the audience he was aiming to reach. 'There were five million people living in Scotland who had rarely seen their lives on the cinema screen', he said. As it turned out, *Gregory's Girl* had a far greater reach than even Forsyth had imagined possible because of the way it celebrated the 'localness' of community life, giving it a universal appeal. But the film also depicted a socialist vision of Britain, one dreamt up by postwar optimists. Forsyth shows a community in transition, moving away from the divisions of Empire and heavy industry towards the service industry. It is no coincidence that Gregory's father (Dave Anderson) is a self-employed driving instructor. Gregory's mother is also entrepreneurial. She runs a pre-school nursery, presumably for the modern working mum, of which she is one, which means Gregory is left to his own devices. Gregory, an '80s style latch-key kid, is seen fixing his own breakfast, one of dog biscuits and toothpaste, with a pineapple smoothie on the side. Forsyth also hilariously highlights the transitional and confused state of Scottish post–feminist culture, one striving for, however clumsily and experimentally, equality not just between classes but between the sexes.

Forsyth chose Cumbernauld as the setting for the film, a modernist scheme constructed in 1955 as an architectural utopia to house the aspirant working class. 'The new-town setting was deliberate', he told journalists after the film was shot. To tell his story he needed, 'a backdrop where nothing was touched or old', the antithesis of the decaying ghettos of urban miserablism from which many of the new town's occupants had been decanted.

Like the miserablist works *Small Faces* (1996) and *Sweet Sixteen* (2002), *Gregory's Girl* (1981) centres on characters going through rites of passage, in this case a group of secondary school pupils on the verge of adulthood. But unlike their miserablist counterparts who are ensnared in violent gangs, Gregory and his friends are free to make their own choices and navigate their way humorously towards adulthood and greater maturity. Although Forsyth claims Gregory's rite of passage is a 'comedy of diversity', the combination of that humour and his affectionate observation of his own culture elevates the film to the universal. As he states, 'I did not make it up... it came from the ground on which I stood.'

Much of the reason *Gregory's Girl* was a resounding success was due to the popularity of the loveable but flawed protagonist, Gregory (John Gordon Sinclair). Gregory has a teenage crush on Dorothy (Dee Hepburn), who is not only beautiful but the best player in the football team, and out of Gregory's league in more ways than one. Forsyth depicts a powerful, independent young woman more interested in gaining status within the all-male football team than pursuing boys. Miserablism reverses this dynamic. The miserablist hero is generally preoccupied by his failing status while the female characters pursue him. Although Gregory will inevitably fail in his mission to capture Dorothy's heart, he will ultimately succeed in the greater quest, learning that love is not about power but compatibility and companionship.

Forsyth's follow-up success *Local Hero* (1983), produced by *Chariots of Fire* producer David Puttnam, put Forsyth on the road to Hollywood. Displaced and in exile from the culture he drew on for material, Forsyth's gentle comedies of manners failed to translate inside the Hollywood system.

Housekeeping (1987), the quirky story of two sisters and their eccentric aunt was drastically re-cut in the edit. An explanatory voiceover was imposed by the studio which flattened Forsyth's comic tone, removing the trademark lightness of touch which had made his other films so popular. Distribution was also delayed on his next film *Being Human* (1994), before it also bombed at the box office after studio interference.

As Forsyth explained in a public talk at the Edinburgh Festival in 2009, he was not alone in his predicament.

> Eighty per cent of directors are happy to work in that system. They are happy to shoot four different endings so the studio can choose one later. It was only because I was seen as this outsider figure that my time there became controversial.

Forsyth returned from exile in America to a new kind of exile in Scotland. His almost unique ability 'to see ourselves' and our nation had been worn down and eroded by his Hollywood experience. His attempt to regain his initial vision in his long awaited and much criticised sequel, *Gregory's Two Girls* (1999), a muddled film much closer to the Kailyard films of outsiders who pretend to know about Scottish culture than to his earlier and fresher films. Forsyth's own story is yet another tale of indigenous talent damaged by inevitable displacement and exile due to a lack of film funding and a poverty of confidence at home. Without a healthy and robust Scottish film industry to back and encourage films on the scale they deserve, the native auteur's trajectory becomes that of the miserablist hero, in Forsyth's case playing itself out in his life rather than in his fiction. Ironically, his next film, which will be his first in 15 years, is rumoured to have the working title of *Exile* and has been 'in development' since 2009.

We are still waiting.

CHAPTER FOUR

The Emergence of the Miserablist Hero

ELEANOR YULE

> Fergus, an old broken shell of a man... a wandering ghost, banished even from himself, from the real self of early years – a prisoner, a sick man, a man with no heart nor appetite for life in him.
>
> *The Brothers* by LAG Strong (1932)

THE MISERABLIST HERO is a wanderer, a dispossessed, displaced man. He emerges from centuries of Scottish working-class oppression and is explored in one of the earliest miserablist films, Scottish director David MacDonald's 1947 adaptation of novelist LAG Strong's book, *The Brothers*. The book was conceived and written during a worldwide economic depression in 1932, the year after work was suspended on the *Queen Mary* due to lack of funds. Although not of Scottish origin, the writer LAG Strong drew on his Irish Protestant heritage in *The Brothers,* transposing it into a hypocritical religious community in the Western Highlands of Scotland, one that creates a tragic paradigm for the film's hero, Fergus Macrea (Maxwell Reed).

> His shoulders stooped; his head was bowed upon his chest; his long ape like arms swung loose... His face seamed and furrowed, showed yellow in the wet slanting light. It was rock-like, melancholy and inscrutable.

Set in the early 19th century during the late period of illicit whisky distillation, the novel and film chart the downfall of Fergus Macrae, an early prototype for the miserablist hero. Fergus resides with his all-male crofting family on the coastal rim scraping a meagre existence from the infertile soil and inclement sea. Many crofting communities had been forced from their land towards the coastal edges due to the Highland Clearances, the resulting population influx putting a strain on natural resources, and a second wave of clearances by concerned landowners inevitably resulted in mass migration.

Historian Tom Devine writes that the Clearances 'bring into particularly sharp focus the titanic conflict between the forces of peasant traditionalism and agrarian rationalism', a kind of early industrialisation of the rural sector. Fergus himself faces the looming possibility that, like John Brown's workers over a century later, his manual skills and physical strength will soon be worthless. His father Hector (Finlay Currie) explains that however hard Fergus labours he will never earn what his brother, John (Duncan Macrea) does from smuggling the family's illicit whisky stills, which they sell to, 'a magistrate, a priest, an innkeeper... and six or seven of the gentry', the very class who impose the heavy excise laws. In the book Strong records Fergus's reaction to his father's judgement of him:

> These words with their weight of certainty, pressed heavily upon Fergus' spirit. Indeed they weighed it down forever.

Fergus is therefore separated from his brother due to his economic impotence, and subsequently divided off from his family, thus creating a personal wound common to nearly all miserablist heroes. This psychic wound does not heal through time, but grows and festers through industrialisation transposing itself onto future generations.

In a powerfully bleak scene demonstrating this generational hatred, not just within their family of origin but also towards their wider community, the Macrea family challenge their arch-rivals and neighbours, the McFarishes, to a duel to settle a dispute. The two family elders duel not with weapons, but with their venomous tongues. What ensues is a round of vitriolic cursing of extraordinary hatred.

'If the grave of your ancestors were to be opened', spits out Hector Macrea, 'a stench of slime and putrifaction would pour forth that would poison and putrefy the whole race of men all over the earth'. In miserablist communities there is no hope of forgiveness or redemption, only an endless cycle of bitterness and resentment and as Macrea goes onto say... 'may you be cursed from your first born to your last born and until the earth vomits back your vile dust'.

It is a clear demonstration of what David Craig identified in 1962 as, 'a partisan bitterness... characteristic of the [Scottish] race' which results in 'an inhuman extreme of partiality, in which positions defined themselves more by violence of opposition than by their positive natures'.

The feuding elders of *The Brothers* make Macbeth's witches look like the Andrews Sisters in this deeply negative vision of a community where kinship, forgiveness and wisdom do not exist. This vision is reinforced by many other miserablist texts, notably Peter McDougall's *Just a Boy's Game* where the narrative is driven by miserablist hero Jake McQuillen's (Frankie Millar) desire to be the toughest Hard Man in town, even tougher than his grandfather, who killed Jake's father, his own son, in a gang fight. Towards the end of the film Jake has a rare instance of epiphany and is ready to forgive his dying grandfather for murdering his father. Hoping to break the cycle of familial hatred he delivers a heart-rending monologue:

Granda, whatever happened between you and my faither doesnae matter, understand? It never bothered me. Those things happen. I've always respected you. I know the game. I'm like yourself. Understand?

His grandfather responds to Jake's entreaty with his dying breath:

I've never been fond of you and when I was younger I could have had you any day.

Even when the miserablist hero finds it in his damaged psyche to forgive and forget and try to move on, forgiveness seems impossible.

These searingly negative visions of family and community are also displayed in Peter Mullan's early short black and white film, *Fridge,* where a tenement community lock up their doors and windows rather than help to rescue a trapped young boy. These depictions of fragmented and suspicious communities are justified by miserablists and passed off as 'realism', defended as the true face of poverty and a reaction to the bogus Tartanry and Highland kinship depicted in *I Know Where I'm Going* and *Brigadoon.*

Feudal disputes have been common to all countries and cultures – the devastation caused by Shakespeare's Montagues and Capulets is a famous example. But Shakespeare uses Romeo and Juliet's tragic tale as a moral polemic warning against the dangers of generational feuding and its resulting destruction of the young and vulnerable. In *The Brothers* and *Just a*

Boy's Game the hero can challenge but never change the powerful grip of the family/communities unjust immorality, and although Fergus's scheming brother John gets his comeuppance in *The Brothers*, it's the powerful gang of smugglers who recycle a technique to enact out their revenge which is most powerfully demonstrated in the opening scenes of the film.

In what must be one of the darkest moments in any miserablist work, they dispatch an informer who has exposed their illicit whisky stills by tying him up, placing floats under his arms and strapping a herring to his head so that a passing goose will dive for the fish and fracture his skull. It's the perfect murder, and one where no one has to deal with the consequences or take responsibility for their actions. Unlike Lady Macbeth, who pays heavily for the blood she imagines on her hands, the bullies in miserablist communities never feel guilt for the rivers of blood they spill:

> The crash of the impact could be heard for half a mile... The iron beak had split his head as a wedge splits a piece of wood, and was buried deep down his gullet. With difficulty they detached the floats, and substituted heavy stones. Then they let go and the goose and informer sank together in a whirl of bubbles to the weedy bottom of the loch.

Much like Munch's *Scream*, the miserablist hero is engulfed within a landscape of mistrust, a moral vacuum he has to navigate in almost total isolation. But he has one reliable companion, the same companion that his modern descendants have come to rely on, his addiction.

Fergus is described as having a 'temptation'. In his case, not surprisingly, it is whisky. His excessive drinking bouts have worn away the lining of his stomach but the taste of self-destruction gives him an almost orgasmic pleasure:

> He gulped down a second measure and a third. A glow spread in the centre of his body. Slowly, like a flower it unfolded, and blossomed hiding his pain away beneath its petals.

Addiction is the key to the miserablist hero's personality. For *Trainspotting*'s Renton (Ewan McGregor) it is heroin, for *The Big Man*'s Dan Scoular (Liam Neeson) it is violence, but alcohol is the drug of choice for the majority, the narrative often centring around a hopeless struggle to control it within the hostile conditions in which the character has to survive.

This is the true and often tragic love affair within miserablism, the relationship between the hero and his addiction, which is why women, and the hero's relationships with them, occupy a slim space in these texts, female characters often appearing only in secondary or supporting roles. This love affair with addiction does not stop the miserablist hero from attracting women. Ironically it only increases his allure, as he is perceived as challengingly unattainable. Although his heart can be broken, it's unlikely he will ever have the maturity or opportunity to truly love in return. This leaves women within miserablism, not just lovers but wives and mothers, locked into a frustrating and irresolvable paradox.

In *The Brothers*, Mary (Patricia Roc), an eye-catching young woman and orphan from Glasgow is taken in by the Macreas. It's not long before she falls for the tortured Fergus, even though she is desired and treated well by the handsome son of a rival crofting family. It is hard to see why Fergus is the object of her desire. Where is the interest? Tortured, repressed and alcoholic, he seems to have little to offer, but within miserablism he is irresistible. Fergus is Mary's addiction and one that, like alcohol for him, will kill her too. Even when Fergus collapses into the heather in a drunken blackout, his mouth damp with vomit, Mary can't help stealing a kiss from his comatose lips.

Not surprisingly, the film ends tragically. Fergus is persuaded by his older brother, who secretly lusts after Mary, that it is his duty to kill her, as she will bring shame on the Macrea name because of her flirtation with the son of a rival crofting family. Fergus, tortured and flawed, does his duty and drowns the lovesick girl. He then commits suicide because he cannot live with the guilt.

There is no redemption, only shame. The sins of the fathers are carried on down the line and transferred to new generations in the form of repressed anger which frequently turns to open violence and aggression, and a deep hostility to hope and any creative solutions.

Although *The Brothers* set the tone for miserablism, it was Scottish auteur Bill Douglas that established it as a cinematic art form and set the miserablist hero loose on his epic journey of thwarted dreams and dispossession.

Douglas is seen by David Martin Jones in his book *Scotland: Global Cinema* as the 'originator of indigenous Scottish cinema', a tradition Martin calls, 'art cinema', linking him to subsequent directors such as Peter Mullan, Lynne Ramsay and David MacKenzie, all considered by Hannah McGill in her *Sight and Sound* article in November 2006 as creators of miserablist works, identifying them as part of, 'an oft-maligned tradition of slum-bound Scottish Miserablism'.

Bill Douglas's bleak but deeply memorable and under-recognised trilogy, *My Childhood* (1972), *My Ain Folk* (1973) and *My Way Home* (1978), like *The Brothers* was shot on black and white film stock, and possesses both the gritty tones of British social realist cinema and the 'poetic realism' of John Grierson's documentaries. Douglas's emergent style is seen as a clear reaction to the candy-coloured Romanticism of the Kailyard films. According to Andrew O'Hagan, Douglas 'mocked the quixotic posturing of a bogus national identity – exploding the tired iron platitudes of family loyalty, couthy neighbours and yer ain fireside.'

Douglas embeds within *The Trilogy* a strong miserablist ethos and mise-en-scène, both through the actions of his young hero Jamie (Stephen Archibald) and the disease instilled within him by his hostile Calvinistic family and community, similar to the forces that destroy Fergus in *The Brothers*.

Douglas' miserablist hero, Jamie, is based on himself and his own very real upbringing in the depths of the '30s depression in the impoverished Scottish east coast mining town of Newcraighall. In the first of the films, *My Childhood*, the brooding seas and infertile lands of the Highlands are replaced with the landscape of industrial decline, one that will take a firm grip within miserablism and relocate itself, through Douglas, into an urban, industrialised context. Many of the same sort of men who mined the coal at Newcraighall were dispossessed crofters from *The Brothers* who had been driven from their homes into Scotland's Central Belt to find work.

In Jamie, Douglas introduces the miserablist hero as another 'rites of passage' character, usually a young boy ripped prematurely from childhood, never having had the chance to fully grow up, mature and express himself within the crushing constraints of Scottish culture. We see this character reappear over the decades in many miserablist works, for example, films in which the miserablist hero is an actual child, as in Lynne Ramsay's *Ratcatcher* (1999), or where the miserablist hero behaves like a child as in Peter McDougall's 1979 television play, *Just a Boys Game*

(1979), and his '90's TV screenplay (which is almost nostalgic miserablism) *Down Among the Big Boys* (1993). This Peter Pan hero, again created by the pen of a Scot (Paul Laverty), is also manifest in Ken Loach's *Sweet Sixteen* (2002), where Liam (Martin Compston) approaches his 16th birthday with his innocence already corrupted by violence, his dreams dashed and on the verge of going to prison for murder.

Douglas' trilogy also highlights one of the major dilemmas for the miserablist hero – how to escape the oppression of the 'mob' or 'gang', or in Jamie's case, the limited, narrow values of his family trying to survive their emotional and economic poverty.

In My Way Home (1978), the final part of the trilogy, in a heart-wrenching scene Jamie tells his father (Paul Kermack) and his step-mother Agnes (Jessie Combe) what he wants to do in life.

> Jamie is standing in the corner of his father's living room, a moody figure. His face is coal black from the pit.
>
> JAMIE: I want to be an artist.
>
> AGNES: And what kind of job is that?
>
> His father and Agnes and Archie stare at him.
>
> AGNES: I've bloody well asked you a question.
>
> The father turns and goes out of the room. He takes himself into the lavatory and shuts the door behind him.

The poker-faced Agnes goes on to bitterly lambast Jamie with what Andrew O'Hagan identifies as 'Calvinistic masochism'.

> An artist? Don't come here with your high falootin' ideas. You go and do [an] honest day's work and get some dirt on your hands. If you were meant to be different you'd have been born different. This is your place in life.

This gives the miserablist hero two choices, to stay and die artistically or metaphorically survive by leaving. Cairns Craig has identified this Scottish tendency to offer no salvation at home as 'nostophobia', and in *Scottish Cinema Now* he defines it:

> Like Jamie... the nostophobe can flourish only by recognition of the fact that s/he is a prisoner in a homeland whose history will produce neurosis unless he/she can escape from that destructive environment.

He adds that, 'nostophobia assumes that the homeland suffers, and suffers uniquely, from a distortion and repression of the self that can only be cured by flight.'

But escape puts off for good the opportunity for the hero to come to terms with and accept his own nationality and therefore reach self-knowledge at home. In the final film of the trilogy, *My Way Home*, completed only months before Scotland's 1979 failed devolution referendum, Jamie finally escapes by joining the army to serve in Egypt.

> In Egypt, Jamie sees other worlds, other cultures, within which he can find acceptance after Scotland's rejection of him: worlds of the imagination, of reading and collecting books, of making films, of experiencing exotic religions and possible love between men ... Jamie, at last, like many of us, has to leave home to home in on himself.
>
> O'HAGAN

Jamie's life in Scotland is presented by Douglas as being bleakly empty of creative activity and also there's an implied rejection of both Douglas's and Jamie's homosexuality. In fact Douglas' own life was very different. Scotland was a place to which he did and could return to make the trilogy as an auteur, although the film's very modest budget came from his tireless patron Mamoun Hassan at the BFI in London.

There's no doubt that Douglas's own time away from Scotland had allowed him to grow and find his own artistic voice, but it was also a voice that was nourished by the culture that formed him.

Like his fictional character Jamie, Douglas did part of his national service in Egypt where he met his life partner Peter Jewell. Jewell not only introduced Douglas to the arts but also encouraged him in 1959 to join Joan Littlewood's Theatre Workshop in Stratford East, as an actor. Littlewood, searching for a place to establish her brand of innovative theatre, far from being exiled from Scotland had tried to stay in it, searching for a theatre in Glasgow, but was forced to move with her company to a London one with cheaper rent. Littlewood's Brechtian way of working with actors and her pioneering improvisational techniques clearly influenced the way Douglas worked with his own cast on the trilogy. He worked with both professional and non-professional actors to produce a heightened but extremely naturalistic performance style for the film which can be seen reflected in later miserablist works, notably Ken Loach's *Sweet Sixteen* (1995) and Lynne Ramsay' *Ratcatcher* (1999).

This 'naturalistic' performance style increases the element of realism within the world of the film, where narrative surprise is often made genuine for the actor during the shoot. The miserablist hero is framed as a universal everyman: the common working man. In Douglas's words, 'I wanted actors who would be humble enough to want to share the same experience in presenting these men.' Douglas discovered that sense of authenticity in Stephen Archibald, the young actor he cast as Jamie, who grew up within the character across the seven years it took to make the trilogy. Archibald, himself from a background of poverty and addiction, eventually died of a heroin overdose. The reality he was cast for was one from which he finally escaped, in his case through drugs, unlike his alter ego who escaped through exile.

This choice of casting as close to reality as possible is both an aesthetic and an economic one. Miserablism is increasingly cheap to produce, even if skilled directors like Douglas, Ramsay and Mullan (who all worked for low fees) manage to create the illusion of a larger budget film. Using actors who are either untrained or less well known is significantly cheaper than using 'stars', who generally expect large fees and luxurious working conditions. Stars also bring their own agenda to any film as well as large audiences. Miserablism needs the anonymity of the unknown or lesser-known actor to add to the veracity of the world they are creating. Their very awkwardness as actors holds a mirror up to nature making it harder to see that the film is a construction. As miserablism is traditionally a low-budget genre it can afford to speak to smaller audiences but can't afford to pay 'named' actors large salaries, and sometimes, as is increasingly the case on micro-budget miserablism, can't pay them at all.

Bill Douglas also established that the path for any miserablist director would be personal and therefore a labour of love. Douglas, like many other miserablist directors, uses a large element of biographical content in the script. He seems to have literally ripped the film from his damaged soul, almost as a form of therapy. As Lindsay Anderson in the foreword to the BFI's Bill Douglas: A Lanternist's Account says:

> Filmmaking was a kind of agony for Bill because, particularly at the start, his films were torn out of himself. And helping to make his films was a kind of agony for his collaborators too.

Although his trilogy went on to win critical acclaim, awards, and is now seen as a classic of Scottish cinema, Douglas spent the rest of his short life deeply frustrated and unsupported by both the Scottish and eventually the UK film industries. It took him eight years to make his next and final feature film *Comrades* (1987) about the Tollpuddle Martyrs, which he struggled to realise against the hostile landscape of Tory rule and trade union collapse. *Comrades* is a more redemptive film with a larger budget, a professional cast and was shot outside Scotland in Dorset and Australia. Douglas, like Mullan and Ramsay, only becomes miserablist when he is working at home.

Douglas was only 54 when he died of cancer, with his best work still to come, just two years younger than Charles Rennie Mackintosh, who at 56, after the completion of the groundbreaking Glasgow School of Art, was forced into exile unable to secure architectural commissions in Scotland. His and Bill Douglas's stories are similar to each other, and similar to many of Scotland's frustrated and under-appreciated sons and daughters. Mackintosh, like Douglas, was eventually killed by his addiction, smoking, and professional disappointment, spending the last years of his life in France painting watercolours rather than producing what could have been his most inspired architectural creations. Twenty-two years after Douglas's death his masterly screenplay of Hogg's classic Confessions of a Justified Sinner is still unproduced. Two of Scotland's most talented sons – their lives like those of the miserablist heroes of their culture.

But what drives these doom-laden scenarios for Jock Tamson's bairns? Do they accurately reflect the reality of life in Scotland for the majority of the population or are they just 'stories' we like to tell ourselves about ourselves? Do we suffer a deeply rooted historical addiction to darkness and dysfunction?

CHAPTER FIVE

The Great Pretenders

ELEANOR YULE

ALTHOUGH SCREENWRITER Peter McDougall wrote for the small screen, most notably for BBC's anthology drama series, *Play for Today*, his collaboration with Scottish director, David Mackenzie, in the '70's produced an unforgettable series of hard-hitting and well-crafted films that put Scottish miserablism on the international map as a force to be reckoned with. Together, McDougall and Mackenzie refined and expanded miserablism by borrowing the panache and scale of the American Western and merging it with the 'gallows' humour of the Greenock pub.

Born in 1947, Peter McDougall came from working-class, protestant stock. Strongly influenced by fellow Greenock born novelist and screenwriter (and, briefly, McDougall's brother-in-law) Alan Sharp, McDougall worked as a housepainter before taking up the pen. Sharp, who relocated to Hollywood after his groundbreaking novel, *A Green Tree in Gedde*, served as an example to McDougall of working-class men who could elevate themselves by telling their own stories.

Sharp, given up by his single mother for adoption to religious parents who worked on the shipyards, went on to live in Los Angeles and marry four times. Sharp had all the necessary ingredients to become a transatlantic miserablist. Once in Hollywood, he developed an aesthetic of his own, one which merged American history with his Scottish miserbalist formation. In his recent *Guardian* obituary, Ronald Bergan commented on Sharp's 'bleakness', and 'cynical sense of destiny', both characteristics of a miserablist ethos.

> Most of his screenplays were written in the 1970s and reflect the era in which America was suffering the effects of the Vietnam War and post-Watergate paranoia. This goes some way to explaining the bleakness and cynical sense of destiny in Sharp's films, which he called 'existential melodramas'.

This merging of miserablist themes within an American context also inspired McDougall to think outside the Caledonian box. McDougall's second screenplay, *Just Another Saturday* (1975), used the miserablist model to tackle the then rising problem of sectarian violence and bigotry along Scotland's west coast. In *Just Another Saturday* Jon Morrison (Jon McNeil) is the young protestant rites of passage hero who is proud to be chosen to swing his mace at the head of the Orange Walk. Through Jon's eyes we experience the thrill of the parade and understand his unquestioning desire to be a part of the 'gang'. It is also through his eyes that we see the increasing drunkenness and underlying violence of his fellow marchers. The film culminates in Jon witnessing violent attacks on Catholic protestors and innocent bystanders by his 'friends', which includes a pensioner being glassed in the face. *Just Another Saturday* goes further than other miserablist texts in deconstructing the miserablist hero. It cracks him open, displays his workings and in Jon's case gives him an awareness and an acceptance of who he is. This rites of passage character is allowed to 'experience' those rites and grow, but not necessarily move on. Jon's journey is existential, a shift of perception rather than reality, but in writing it McDougall passes the ball to other writers by opening up the possibility for them to develop a way forward. Here for the first time is the possibility that the miserablist hero could evolve, change and not remain doomed but learn valuable lessons and take action to change things.

Powerful, brave and relevant, *Just Another Saturday* was internationally recognised, winning the Prix Italia, and establishing McDougall and Mackenzie as an invincible double act. While Thatcher made her claims that poverty was eradicated and community no longer existed, McDougall and Mackenzie's films shouted their existence from the rooftops of the run down pubs and wastelands of the post-industrial schemes.

Elephants Graveyard (1976) followed a year later starring a young Billy Connolly, fresh from his stage hit in the *Great Northern Welly Boot Show*. Connolly, at the time struggling with a real life drink problem of his own, plays Jody, an unemployed loser with a fertile imagination. One of the 'redundant' skilled working class, his pride forces him to act out an elaborate charade. He accepts his wife's homemade 'pieces' and tells her he's off to work in a factory. Instead he hides out in the hills behind Greenock rather than admit he is unemployed. Early in the film we are told that Jody's wife is expecting his first 'fictional' pay cheque so his period of 'escape' is about to come to an end. While in hiding he meets an alter ego, Bunny (Jon Morrison) who, it turns out, has the same idea. The men, partners in a relatively benign crime, spend the day together, talking, philosophising and connecting. It is a funny and touching drama with only a slim hope at the end that the future may be rosy. Although physically absent in the film, the female characters have a strong hold on the men – they are seen as 'other'. Even though they are wives and lovers they are depicted, as in other miserablist texts, as responsible (often nagging) 'mothers', or parents of errant 'boys'. McDougall's miserablist hero may be evolving but he does not grow up.

Nowhere is this dynamic better played out than in what is arguably the pinnacle of McDougall's collaboration with Mackenzie, *Just a Boys' Game* (1979). Set in the 'noir' alleys, shipyards and subterranean bars of Greenock, miserablist hero and charmer Dancer Dunnichy (Ken Hutchison) gets hopelessly sucked into the machinations of a local knife gang and meets a tragic end.

Dancer, like many other miserablist heroes and all McDougall's protagonists, is a Peter Pan character, a boy who does not want to grow up. Even though he is physically mature and has children of his own he also fits the rites of passage miserablist archetype perfectly. As his name suggests, he believes he can dance through life, eternally escaping responsibility and the consequences of his irresponsible and hedonistic actions.

Dancer is employed in the declining shipyards but earns too little to comfortably support both his small family and his drinking habit. His gaunt, anxious, chain-smoking wife, Jane (Katherine Stark), waits at home, nursing her grudges and waiting to box his ears on his return from his weekend binges in the local pub. In a scene from the film, loaded with McDougallesque black humour, Dancer's small children, bored with witnessing the same pattern of events and far more mature than their parents, ignore their histrionics by turning on the TV, preferring to watch an Open University lecture on quantum physics instead.

In a symbolic and violent end to the film, Dancer's neck is broken when he blindly runs into a steel rope while being chased by a gang member along the docks. The weight of industry breaks the spirit of the boy, the steel severing the head from the heart. Here McDougall brings hope for his miserablist hero to an abrupt end, shutting down the glimmer of possibility and promise that Jon's earlier existential shift away from violence and bigotry had brought in *Just Another Saturday*. Dancer only has one chance and fails – he is not allowed to dance again. Like a Calvinist morality tale, he is struck down and punished for his sins, crushed flat by the fist of a cruel and cold God.

McDougall's writing re-energised miserbalism by injecting it with a darkly comic tone born of acute observation, and drawn from local folk tales, urban myths and the 'craic' of west-coast male drinking culture. The miserablists that followed often lacked the observation, wit or the innovation and sparkle of the McDougall-Mackenzie stamp. *Just a Boys' Game* was the last film McDougall and Mackenzie made together before Mackenzie, like so many directors before him, tried his hand in Hollywood. The story is a familiar one. Mackenzie's craftsmanship and sensibility failed to shine within the homogenised studio system. His decade in the States yielded a clutch of lacklustre movies. McDougall, meanwhile, continued on his own, his miserablist vision more mellow but lacking Mackenzie's sharp edge. His later work, *Shoot for the Sun* (1986), *Down Where the Buffalo Go* (1988) and *Down Among the Big Boys* (1993), the last made during the post-Thatcher era, lacked the power, punch and relevance of his earlier work.

In time, McDougall gravitated towards the two options available to Scottish screenwriters, and the ones favored by film financiers as safe bets – the Kailyard and a new twist, 'faux miserablism', which emerged in the post-Thatcher era and thrived under the Blair leadership, and which nurtured and encouraged a slick and empty repackaging of socialist values. A kind of simulacrum, a pretence, Blair's ideology smelled like socialism, it looked like socialism but the core values were missing. The same was true of 'faux miserablism'. It looked like miserablism and was sold as miserablism but it was empty of the sharp social message and political relevance of its predecessors.

Gillies MacKinnon's razor gang biopic *Small Faces* (1996), Ken Loach's uncompromisingly bleak tale of a doomed teenager *Sweet Sixteen* (2002), and Glasgow company Raindog's nihilistic tale of tragic junkie lovers *Wasted* (2009), all seek to regurgitate the horror and pointlessness of miserablism but without the heart, the humour or the immediacy of its earlier incarnations.

More importantly, faux miserablism offers no distinctive stylistic innovation, remaining stubbornly linear in its plot lines and naturalistic in its visual style. These films allow no hope and no future for their protagonists within a Scottish context, despite that context having changed substantially since Bill Douglas's *Trilogy* nearly 40 years before, where the impact of the post-industrial economy was a genuinely pressing issue. If cinema, like dreaming, represents the unconscious of our nation, what do these more recent films say about the true state of our collective psyches?

In 2003, an initiative known as Advance Party was created to develop a trilogy of films as a collaboration between SIGMA, Scottish producer Gillian Berrie's company, and Lars Von Triers's Zentropa studio in Denmark. Berrie was drawn to Zentropa's inspirational and egalitarian studio model and its diverse filmic output, believing the Danish methodology and that country's ability to produce original, economic films with popular appeal could transfer to Scotland.

Among Zentropa's early successes were the incest story *Festen* (1998), the risqué comedy *The Idiots* (1997), and female director Lone Schefig's delightful ensemble romance *Italian for Beginners* (2000). Von Trier himself had created a highly original film in and about Scotland. *Breaking the Waves* (1996) is stylistically innovative, blending noir with magic realism and boasts, unlike miserablism, a memorable female character in Bess McNeill (Emily Watson), who, although her journey is ultimately tragic, is explored in psychic depth. In *Breaking the Waves*, Von Trier also deconstructs and exposes the underlying repressed religious values which dominate miserablism. Von Trier's bold innovation and experimentation is perhaps what Berrie believed could shift some of the stubborn polarity within Scottish filmmaking and influence a broadening of its dramatic range.

Despite this ambition to break out of the miserablist mould, the first film to emerge from the Advance Party initiative, *Red Road* (2006), written by the English director Andrea Arnold, was categorised by film critic Hannah McGill as falling into the miserablist tradition, even though she acknowledges the film as engaging and well–made.

> *Red Road* remains... moody, starless, admired abroad but too forbidding to attract wide audiences at home. Though Arnold herself is

English, her film fits (un)comfortably into an oft-maligned tradition of slum-bound Scottish miserablism that stretches from Bill Douglas to Lynne Ramsay, David Mackenzie and Peter Mullan.

Although *Red Road*, like *Breaking the Waves*, had a well-defined female central character and a mildly redemptive ending, the setting of a crumbling modernist scheme and the general ennui among its central characters casts the familiar grey-tinted shadow of miserablism. Similarly, the follow up, *Donkeys* (2010), by the inspired Scots director Morag McKinnon, also followed the spirit of humorous nihilism and centred around one of miserablism's favourite themes, the 'sins of the father'. Here again, even with Danish influence, the film ends with the message that making amends for past errors remains too problematic within a Scottish context.

Most recently miserablism has seeped into horror, another genre which sells easily and can be relatively cheap to produce, a genre which was in part created by females to explore their unconscious, and has now evolved, within cinema, into a genre which is more often about women *being* exploited through sex and violence. Colm McCarthy's film *Outcast* (2010) is genre-busting. It uniquely combines miserablism and horror. It uses the provenance of miserablism to give the film its unique selling point. A horror film set on a council estate, *Outcast* possesses all 17 of the key characteristics of miserablism. It is in fact a perfect example of the miserablist genre, even if it looks like a horror film, it was marketed as a horror film, and it sold as a horror film. It was generally confusing to its audience, however. Another simulacrum, inferior to the original. The message of *Outcast* is where the film most conspicuously reveals its miserablist roots – the young can never be free, our dysfunctional culture cannot be escaped and no matter how hard we try we are ultimately doomed to failure. Darkness will always conquer love.

Simulacra have also affected miserablism's polar opposite – the Kailyard. Just after the millennium the saturation of miserablist screenplays within Scotland created a backlash among Scottish film development executives and mainstream Scottish audiences. There followed a determined effort among both film and television commissioners to actively fund positive depictions of Scotland, which spawned a revival of Kailyard confections which included the disappointingly lacklustre *The Stone of Destiny* (2008), Ken Loach's homage to Ealing studio's *Whisky Galore!*, *The Angels' Share* (2012), and *The Decoy Bride* (2012), a concoction of Kailyard clichés.

It seems apt then that the greatest innovator in the miserablist canon, Peter McDougall, is currently writing screenplays for remakes of Ealing comedies, *The Maggie* and *Whisky Galore!* McDougall, once the great innovator, now forced into the ranks of the Great Pretenders.

CHAPTER SIX

Wholeheartedness:
The Way Forward?

ELEANOR YULE and DAVID MANDERSON

AT THE ENTRANCE to the newly refurbished Hillhead Underground, a large mural greets passengers entering the station from the street or coming up the elevator to leave it. Alasdair Gray's subway art, completed in 2012, confronts his native city, and by extension his nation and his culture, with a rich, funny, sinister, intricate, complex and diverse portrait of itself. In a country small enough to know or know of everybody, recognisable characters include Liz Lochhead and her husband and Gray's father and son. The streets and buildings of the area are identified and named. Glasgow's modernist gothic architecture sprawls over the head of the hill, bisected by roads and studded with university towers and housing blocks, the whole work intricately labelled and tagged, not so much a map as the living story of an area, inspiring wonder and curiosity in the viewer in a way that only a guide to real people in their place can. The point is not to recognise the beauty of Glasgow's west end (which Gray has also decorated in other spots, such as the Òran Mór church at the top of Byres Road and the Ubiquitous Chip restaurant in Ashton Lane), but to show Glasgow, above all, as a place made up of people and their lives rather than monuments and buildings, a human face, ever-changing, laughing and crying, showing dignity, preserving memory, loving and living and marking the passing of age and emotion.

In tiled panels on either side of the main mural a remarkable number of archetypal characters are portrayed. They include the usual miserablist figures – bonny fighters, urban foxes and merry devils. But alongside them, equal to them and rubbing shoulders with them are lovely mums, independent women, bold explorers, culture vultures, queer fishes, lucky dogs, birds of paradise and hopeful children. Gray provides a score of archetypes where the miserablist tradition provides two or three.

Of all contemporary Scottish artists, Gray has had the least to do with the false binary of Scotland as either Kailyard or miserablist. He incorporates the city and the country, the dark and the couthy, the emotional, the shameful and the proud within his multiform vision of Scotland the nation. He has consistently refused the labels of Tartanry and Clydesidism without ever rejecting their original worth as both a contemporary Romantic and an artist concerned with the socially real and the realistically magic. His political ideal is a socialist Scottish independent nation in its fiction, its art and its reality, healthy and vibrant in the diversity and richness of talent among its 'folk' – always Gray's preferred term for people. 'Work as if you are in the early days of a better nation', now carved on the Canongate wall of the Scottish Parliament, is taken from the frontispiece of his *Unlikely Stories, Mostly* (1983). Gray attributes the line to Canadian author Dennis Lee, but it readily sums up Gray's own life, work and aspirations.

Born and raised in the post-war optimism of the welfare state, and associated through his father, Tom Gray, with the walking movements in the nearby country and the assertion of ordinary people's rights to wayfare, Alasdair Gray, of all living Scottish artists, has coined new myths for Scotland without dispensing with the old ones. He invests objects drawn from real and fantastical everyday life with mythic significance – working men's bunnets, pigeons, dragons, mermaids, unicorns, squirrels. He has always had space for the miserablist heritage as an important part of our shared legacy, one not to be censored, and has long been a friend and admirer of miserablist writer James Kelman. Nor would he agree with the label of miserablism, or with any other label. The point of Gray's art is that it seeks to be entire, to encompass all things, everywhere, including what it is to be an ordinary citizen of a small nation, and to show what his world has in common with, and is distinct from, everyone else's. *Lanark*, his break-through novel in 1981, is miserablist to its core, with its vision of a dark, timeless city, haunted by people with degenerative diseases such as dragonhide and twittering, and an elite institution that feeds off the masses. But like Hogg's *Confessions*, *Lanark* is greater than any single element, too big in its scope and ambition to settle for one message. 'Oh! This is hell!' Lanark exclaims as he finally understands the ugliness and despair of Unthank, the city where he has arrived with no memory. But in *Lanark*, unlike miserablism, there is always a way out, even if it does lead to another hell, as

Lanark finds in a graveyard where he is consumed by a giant mouth. Brooding and sombre though Gray's epic is, it is also hopeful, speculative, surreal, socially real, happy, grieving, comic and even, in places, optimistic. It ends with a vision of the end of the world that seems to wash away all that has been before, and allow a new, better universe to be created.

Andy Murray, Scotland's (and Britain's) Wimbledon tennis singles champion, is a son of the middle classes. Raised in Dunblane, he was one of the children who hid under their desks while gunman Thomas Campbell entered Dunblane primary school and gunned down 16 infants and one adult, their teacher. It was an early brush with a disturbed individual taking revenge for his self-imposed trap, his outraged sense of isolation and injustice compelling him to take not just his own life but also the lives of innocent children. From an early age Murray was noticed for his competitiveness. His talent, but also – more importantly – his desire to win was spotted early by his trainers and at 16 he was whisked off to Barcelona to train at the Sanchez-Casal tennis academy. It was an exile he has described as 'a big sacrifice', possibly of his youth. Returning to start playing seriously on the junior and then the professional circuits, he seemed to possess a very un-Scottish desire to win, as well as the ability to. But, with the hopes of the British public, the pressures of the Scottish and British press, and the traditional miserablist Scottish tendency to self-destruct resting on his thin frame, his prospects of success seemed always in doubt. The question was never whether he would win Wimbledon, but how narrowly he would lose it, following the path of noble defeat trodden by earlier British tennis darlings like Tim Henman and David Lloyd, and by all Scottish international football teams. At the same time, commentators noticed something different about Murray, and they didn't much like it. He didn't smile, he kept his head down, he seemed unwilling to make eye contact, and wouldn't or couldn't deliver the telling sound bite. Perhaps his will to win, obvious on court, somehow lacked the killer's edge in the studio. Perhaps this inability to seem at ease in interviews betrayed a deep interior lack of confidence. In fact perhaps he was altogether too Scottish, too much a miserablist, with his dourness, darkness and lack of charm, to ever be able to win. Or, worse than being a loser, he might turn out to be an ungracious winner, something the media would never forgive him for.

It was the classic example of several stereotypes being unloaded onto the shoulders of a young man trying to deal with massive media pressure and to perfect his game at the same time. Murray more than any other sportsman had to grow up in front of the cameras, and his development from stringy but powerful teenager who tended to fade in the last set to a lean and rangy man with the strength, energy and desire to overcome every opponent took place in the public arena where the media cast a cynical eye on him for signs of failure, year on year. Everyone knew he had the talent and the stamina, but did he have the personality, the slickness, the charisma, to be a real hero?

Murray answered his doubters not through victory, but in the most unexpected way. He showed his vulnerability in defeat, shedding tears in front of the crowd and the cameras when beaten by Roger Federer in the 2012 Wimbledon final. It was the turning point of his career. The shy, introverted sportsman had shared something that had seemed buried deep. Far from being afraid to show his emotions, he shared them in the most public and intimate way. Suddenly he was the darling of the British networks, his new popularity assisted by the fact that he was now beginning to genuinely challenge the top professionals. One month later he beat Federer to take Olympic gold, and one year later beat world number one Novak Djokovic in straight sets to win Wimbledon.

Wholeheartedness, an approach to thinking and life recently championed by academic Brene Brown, is a quality both Gray the artist and Murray the sportsman share. It is not the opposite of miserablism and it does not deny pessimism, but it demands that feelings of shame, guilt, envy, jealousy and anger are not repressed, are not allowed to fester, but are forced into the open where they can be considered, understood and so forgiven. It encompasses darkness and also many other things, including happiness, health, friendship, love and physical and mental wellbeing. All are seen as different parts of the whole of human experience. Vulnerability is the key. Admitting one's own sense of shame, failure or lack of self-esteem, and allowing oneself to experience the resulting pain and sorrow – to feel it as well as comprehend it – opens the person to the possibility of renewal, and success. In miserablist fiction, the dark hero may suffer loss of employment and social status, get drunk or starve or inject himself with drugs, and rage against injustice, but he rarely feels. He cannot admit shame or shed tears because miserablism cannot allow recovery. In miserablist screen drama, emotion can be so far from the experience of the characters that they are sometimes mere cyphers, men that walk and talk and growl their way through a series of confrontations, their words and actions rendered meaningless. Gray has always known this is not enough. After Duncan Thaw's mother dies he suffers hallucinations of her that torment him, especially when he falls ill. But when he meets an old friend of his mother's on the bus, he realises that Mary Thaw had a past of her own long before marriage and children:

> But only a few old people remembered her youth nowadays and soon both her youth and her age would be wholly forgotten. He thought 'Oh no! No!' and felt for the only time in his life a pang of pure sorrow without any rage or self-pity in it. He could not weep, but a berg of frozen tears floated near his surface, and he knew that berg floated in everyone, and wondered if they felt it as seldom as he did.

Murray allowed his own barrier against the shame of defeat to break in public and in that moment was transformed in the eyes of the public, to the extent that he is now a national – both Scottish and British – hero. It wasn't so much his later victory as that moment of vulnerability that sealed his reputation as a world champion capable of scaling heights no one else had dared to attempt. The question as to whether Murray will support Scotland as an independent country or as an entity within the United Kingdom in the forthcoming referendum is irrelevant. The point is not how a tennis champion votes, but what Scotland will make of an example of a Scotsman who has become a true hero by showing us not his strength, his anger, or his resentment, but his tears and through his weeping gained victory. Murray recalls older heroes, the Greeks of ancient myth, Ulysses, Theseus or Perseus, in this moment, rather than the miserablist ones, torn from their worlds and addicted to the thing that keeps them where they are, whom Scotland has more often brought into the world. Gray has always sought heroes of this kind in his art, valuing qualities like dignity, warmth, friendliness and respect for themselves and for others in his characters in his fiction and his art. His men prickle with shame, blush with embarrassment, stammer and struggle to talk but still find ways to cope with their lives, and even to love. They discover wholehearted ways of living, just like Murray discovered wholehearted winning. Could Scotsmen like these replace our miserablist models?

Scotland needs to become a wholehearted nation both in life and in the art which represents it. This involves supporting and nurturing our artists, understanding them and encouraging them to break rules in their mythmaking. The most difficult rule of all to break is the showing and sharing of the vulnerability of the main male character. And lead characters need not be male. The lovely mums, independent women and hopeful children are full of stories too. There has always been more than one story to tell, more than one kind of hero, and telling many different kinds of tales will not involve us in selling out, but will embrace wholeheartedness in Scottish fiction, just as its greatest writers and artists – Hogg, Scott, Stevenson, Gray – have always done. Artists themselves need to be encouraged to fail in order to understand and accept their own limitations, but each time to fail a little better, and so constantly improve their art.

Better funding is the mechanism to allow this. With a great tradition in realism and also in documentaries, we are a nation of natural storytellers. Let's celebrate this and the richness of what we already have while at the same time encouraging greater diversity. This trend is already apparent, not just in terms of what writers write about but the new forms they are using to do it. Many artists – writers, filmmakers and visual artists – are now moving into different fields as new online and hybrid forms emerge, or are coming together to work in arts that cross over. This has partly been brought about by the digital revolution in publishing, but also by a sense of restlessness and an urgent awareness of the need for change.

AL Kennedy's recent foray into stand-up comedy is one example of this, while the flood of spoken word events, launches, networks, festivals, slams and performance poetry and prose have burst open the doors supposedly separating the written from the spoken word and the writer from the performance and the audience. Not only do these barriers no longer exist, these experiments rediscover the fact that they never did in the first place. When James Hogg filled up with whisky before speaking at his debating club, or trudged from Glasgow to Paisley with Robert Tannahill to declaim his verse to the crowds assembled at the Braes, he was doing exactly what Scottish writers are doing now, which is to travel and perform at gig after gig like musicians are supposed to. As television, radio and film become more and more accessible and cheaper to make, poets, prose writers and musicians are making their own programmes and learning how to distribute them. In the field of comedy, Billy Connolly, who once led the exodus of other artists from the miserablist fate of trying to make a living in the arts in Scotland in the '70s, still shows the way. He once said that the reason for the success of his comedy was that it 'boldly went where no man had gone before'. Connolly above all has revealed and shared his vulnerability, night after night in his shows. He has always taken the risk, and his recent announcement of his Parkinson's Disease and his fight with prostate cancer is another example, perhaps his greatest and his last, of his ability to show his weakness, his fear, his depression and his shame and, by making them into material for laughter, heal himself and all of us.

Connolly has regularly been the target of abuse by the Scottish press. Locally popular when he was half of the Humblebums, the Scottish media's doyen when he broke through with his *Solo Concert* double album and beloved by them while his fame stayed based in Scotland, he came to be regarded with dislike and suspicion when real success hit with the Michael Parkinson interviews and successful London and international tours. As a result, he went into exile – that non-place that miserablism doesn't recognise – returning only years later, by then married to Pamela Stephenson, to live in Perthshire. Scotland does not do well by its famous sons and daughters, and they do not always go away because things are better elsewhere. It's time too that we stopped sending our successes away and then blaming them for turning their backs on us. Success in Scotland can never have much meaning to a huge audience, so those who do seek greater renown and recognition must travel abroad to find it. Those who have been successful in this quest should be welcomed back, in the hope that some of this international appeal rubs off on the rest of us, so that we can learn from the experience. Connolly, an international star who has never forgotten who he is, is dealing with prostate cancer as he has dealt with other seemingly impossible challenges, such as being a Glaswegian comic on an international stage. He is meeting the challenge by foregrounding his vulnerability, by placing his accent, his nature, and now his illness, stage centre.

In October 2013, two new Scottish films, *Sunshine on Leith* and *Filth*, premiered in Edinburgh. The first, a feel-good musical based on the songs of The Proclaimers, deals neither with the toffs nor the neds – Auld Reekie's two miserablist stereotypes – and instead shows us the lives of the middling folk, the young men and women and their fathers and mothers who make up the vast majority of the population, people living out their lives in a real place in a real time. A piece of advertising for Scotland the brand it may be, with many moments of mawkishness and sentimentality, but it is also a celebratory anti-miserablist film deliberately set in a location better known for its gothic or elitist connotations. In the city of dualities, duality is for once avoided in a narrative that concentrates on relationships, while arch-miserablist actor and director Peter Mullan shows what he can do by playing an ordinary, altogether human and humane character who makes mistakes, learns and understands, shows love, like, anger and empathy in his engagement with the world but at no time confronts it in extremes of love or hate. He is neither saviour nor outcast, tragically lost saint nor bitterly wise sinner, but a man concerned with and part of his family, his place and his community, his place in his society, no more and no less. *Filth*, adapted from the Irvine Welsh novel of the same name, goes for the miserablist jugular with a fierce box-ticking of miserablism's traits. Bruce Robertson is ripped from his family, a failed brother and father. Addiction to alcohol, cocaine, pornography and junk food are his driving forces. His community is in permanent collapse as fat, pasty-faced Edinburghers munch pies, pastries and chips near Edinburgh castle; women barely exist, or exist merely as cyphers to react with hatred to his fury or sympathy to his despair; secrets, lies and unforgiven deeds haunt all his memories, fantasies and relationships. *Filth* plays each of the miserablist cards with increasing desperation as it loses narrative power and coherence, becoming by its end a parody of itself, a series of shock tactics designed to distract the audience from the fact that it isn't working, despite a strong performance by James McAvoy in the lead role. *Sunshine on Leith* and *Filth* represent the two ends of the spectrum, Kailyard and miserablist. The big difference from a century ago is that now it is the miserablist end of the spectrum that is the false stereotype sold overseas to international consumers, the extreme MacDiarmid would have railed against, the stereotype that shows us not as we might be in all our infinite possibilities, but as we're condemned to be in the eyes of the world.

With the independence referendum now facing us, the time to decide what stories to tell about ourselves, and why, is now. It's no longer enough to tolerate the stereotypical because that's what gets commissioned in

London, or to make the most shocking, sentimental or traditional story we can because that's what we're supposed to be like. The creative industries of film, television, theatre and literature in the new Scotland will be one of its biggest employers and will demand diversity, while the process towards political and cultural independence, whatever the outcome of the forthcoming ballot, will continue.

The question now is not whether we want our own identity, but do we really want change? And are we capable of doing it in a Scottish context? Are we to be forever satisfied with our miserablist heritage or can we move on and move out beyond our self-imposed limitations? Can we expand not just our imaginations but our culture? Can we become different from the way we are?

Further Reading

Chapter One

Bold, Alan, *MacDiarmid*, John Murray, 1988.

Bourke, Joanna, *Dismembering the Male: Men's Bodies, Britain, and the Great War*, University of Chicago Press, 1996.

Brown, George Douglas, *The House with the Green Shutters*, Polygon, 2005.

Brown, Rhona in *Kailyard and Scottish Literature* (Ed. Andrew Nash), Rodopi, 2007.

Burgess, Moira, *Imagine a city: Glasgow in fiction*, Argyll Publishing, 1998.

Craig, Cairns, *Fearful Selves* in 'The Modern Scottish Novel: Narrative and the National Imagination', EUP, 2002.

Devine, Tom, *The Scottish Nation: 1700–2000*, Penguin, 2000.

Gardiner, Michael, *From Trocchi to Trainspotting: Scottish Critical Theory Since 1960*, Edinburgh University Press, 2006.

Garside, Peter, *Introduction*, 'The Private Memoirs and Confessions of a Justified Sinner', Stirling/North Carolina.

Hay, George MacDougall, *Gillespie*, Canongate, 2001.

Hind, Archie, *The Dear Green Place*, Birlinn, 2001.

Kelman, James, *The Busconductor Hines*, Polygon, 2007.

Kelman, James, *Not Not While the Giro*, Polygon, 2007.

Lochhead, Liz, *Mary Queen of Scots Got Her Head Chopped Off*, Nick Hern Books, 2009.

McGill, Patrick, *The Rat-Pit*, Birlinn, 1999.

McIlvanney, William, *Strange Loyalties*, Hodder & Stoughton, 1991.

MacMillan, Hector, *The Sash (My Father Wore)*, Molendiner, 1974.

Muir, Edwin, *Scottish Journey*, Mainstream, 1996.

Murray, Charles, *Hamewith*, Aberdeen University Press, 1979.

Parker, Philip, *The Art and Science of Screenwriting*, Intellect, 2nd edn. 2006.

Welsh, Irvine, *Trainspotting*, Vintage, 1994.

Chapter Two

Banks, Iain, *Complicity*, Abacus, 2013.

Brown, Gordon, *Falling*, Fledgling Books, 2009

Buchan, John, *The Thirty-Nine Steps*, Wordsworth Classics, 1993.

Devine, Tom, *Scotland's Empire: 1600–1815*, Penguin, 2004.

Eliot, T. S., *The Waste Land*, Norton & Co., 2004.

Galloway, Janice, *Foreign Parts*, Vintage, 1995.

Gunn, Neil, *The Drinking Well*, Polygon, 2006.

Harvie, Christopher, *Scotland and Nationalism*, Allen and Unwin, 1977.

Hogg, James, *Altrive Tales featuring a 'Memoir of the Author's Life'*. Stirling/North Carolina, 2005.

Kelly, Stuart, *Scott-Land: The Man Who Invented a Nation*, Polygon, 2011.

Kelman, James, *Not Not While the Giro*, Polygon, 2007.

McArthur, Colin, *Scotch Reels*, BFI, 1982.

MacDiarmid, Hugh, *A Drunk Man Looks at the Thistle*, Polygon, 2008.

McIlvanney, William, *Laidlaw*, Canongate, 2013.

MacPherson, James, *The Poems of Ossian*, Edinburgh University Press, 1996.

Manderson, David, *Lost Bodies*, Kennedy and Boyd, 2011.

Petrie, Duncan, *Screening Scotland*, BFI, 2000.

Sexton, Sue Reid, *Mavis's Shoe*, Waverley Books, 2011.

Simons, J., David, *The Credit Draper*, Two Ravens, 2008.

Smith, Iain Crichton, Selected *Stories*, Carcanet, 1990.

Thompson, Douglas, *Ultrameta*, Eibonvale Press, 2009.

Welsh, Irvine, *The Acid House*, Norton, 1995.

Wilson, John (attributed), *Extracts from Gosschen's Diary No.1*, Gothic Short Stories (David Blair ed.), Wordsworth Editions, 2002.

Chapter Three

Das, Lina, 'Not-so-braveheart', *Daily Mail*, http://www.dailymail.co.uk/tvshowbiz/article-1223968/, October 2009.

Griffin, Annie, *Annie Griffin: Talk of the Town*, the Scotsman, 6 February 2009.

James, Oliver, *Affluenza*, Vermilion, 2007.

Martin, Neill, *Friend or Foe: Hospitality and Threshold in Scottish Tradition*, http://www.ed.ac.uk/polopoly_fs/1.64000!/1.64000!/fileManager/FriendorFoe.pdf.

Miller, Phil, *Life, Exile and Being Human, by Bill Forsyth*, www.heraldscotland.com/life-exile-and-being-human, June 2009.

Miller, Phil, *Relocation of drama first step toward Scots hub*, Herald Scotland, 29 March 2012, http://www.heraldscotland.com/news/home-news/relocation-of-drama-first-step-towards-scots-hub.

McArthur, Colin, *Brigadoon, Braveheart and the Scots*, MacMillan, 2003
Powell, Michael, *A Life in Movies*, Faber, 2000.
Sillars, Jane, *Admitting the Kailyard* in 'Scottish Cinema Now' (eds. Murray, Farley, Stoneman), Cambridge Scholars, 2009.
Scorsese, Martin, foreword to *On Film Making* (Mackendrick, Alexander), Faber, 2005.
Wilkinson, Richard and Pickett, Kate, *The Spirit Level: Why Equality is Better for Everybody*, Penguin, 2010.

Chapter Four

Craig, David, 'The New Poetry of Socialism', *New Left Review*, Winter 1962.
Craig, Cairns, 'Nostophobia' in *Scottish Cinema Now* (eds. Murray, Farley, Stoneman), Cambridge Scholars, 2009.
Devine, Tom, *The Highland Clearances*, http://www.ehs.org.uk, Spring 1987.
Martin-Jones, David, *Scotland: Global Cinema*, Oxford University Press, 2009.
O'Hagan, Andrew, 'Homing', *Bill Douglas: A Lanternist's Account* (eds. Dick, Noble, Petrie), BFI, 1993.
Strong, LAG, *The Brothers*, Chatto and Windus, 1970.

Chapter Five

Bergan, Ronald, 'Alan Sharp obituary', *The Guardian*, 14 February 2013.
McGill, Hannah, *The Times* BFI *50th London Film Festival: Mean Streets*, 'Sight and Sound', November 2006.

Chapter Six

Brown, Brene, *Daring Greatly: the Power of Vulnerability*, Portfolio Penguin, 2013.
Gray, Alasdair, *Lanark*, Canongate Books, 2007.

Caledonian Dreaming: The Quest for a Different Scotland
Gerry Hassan
ISBN: 978 1 910021 32 3 PBK £11.99

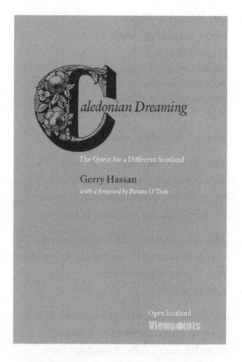

Caledonian Dreaming: The Quest for a Different Scotland offers a penetrating and original way forward for Scotland beyond the current independence debate. It identifies the myths of modern Scotland, describes what they say and why they need to be seen as myths. Hassan argues that Scotland is already changing, as traditional institutions and power decline and new forces emerge, and outlines a prospectus for Scotland to become more democratic and to embrace radical and far-reaching change.

Hassan drills down to deeper reasons why the many dysfunctions of British democracy could dog an independent Scotland too. With a non-partisan but beady eye on society both sides of the border, in this clever book here are tougher questions to consider than a mere Yes/No.
POLLY TOYNBEE, writer and journalist, *The Guardian*

A brilliant book unpacking the political narratives that have shaped modern Scotland in order to create a space to imagine anew. A book about Scotland important to anyone, anywhere, dreaming a new world.
STEPHEN DUNCOMBE, author

There could be no better harbinger of [...] possibilities than this bracing, searching, discomfiting and ultimately exhilarating book.
FINTAN O'TOOLE

On Being a Man: Four Scottish Men in Conversation

Sandy Campbell, John Carnochan,
Pete Seaman, David Torrance.
Preface by Gerry Hassan
ISBN: 978 1 910021 33 0 PBK £7.99

Men of Scotland, speak up!

The silences and evasions of too many men in our society contribute to and magnify the problems we face in relation to individual and collective behaviour.

Men have to start speaking up as men, changing themselves and challenging other men to take responsibility.
GERRY HASSAN

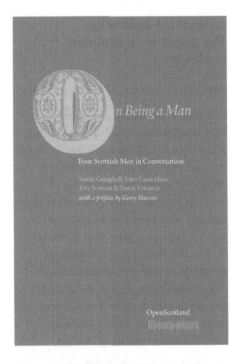

On Being a Man brings together four men to consider the condition of Scottish men, reflect on their own backgrounds and experiences, and confront some of the most difficult issues men face. These include the changing roles of men in Scottish society and the role of work and employment.

What it means to be a man today is very different from forty years ago: in terms of expectations, relationships, how men relate to partners, bring up children and what constitutes a modern family. However, there is a dark side of Scottish masculinity – seen in the drinking and the violent, abusive behaviour of some Scots men and this book addresses this directly, getting into issues many of us often shy away from confronting.

This thoughtful book draws on the wide-ranging voices of journalist, writer and broadcaster, David Torrance; founder of a youth employment and mentoring charity, Sandy Campbell; public health researcher, Pete Seaman; and former policeman and head of the violence reduction unit, John Carnochan.

Blossom:
What Scotland Needs to Flourish
Lesley Riddoch
ISBN: 978 1 908373 69 4 PBK £11.99

Weeding out vital components of
Scottish identity from decades of
political and social tangle is no mean
task, but it's one journalist Lesley
Riddoch has undertaken.

Dispensing with the tired, yo-yoing
jousts over fiscal commissions, devo
something-or-other and EU in-or-out,
Blossom pinpoints both the buds of
growth and the blight that's holding
Scotland back. Drawing from its
people and history, as well as the
experience of the Nordic countries
and the author's own passionate
and outspoken perspective, this is
a plain-speaking but incisive call to
restore equality and control to local
communities and let Scotland flourish.

*Not so much an intervention in the
independence debate as a heartfelt
manifesto for a better democracy.*
THE SCOTSMAN

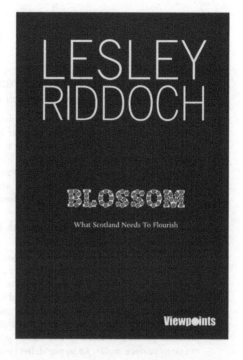

Details of these and other books published by Luath Press can be found at:
www.luath.co.uk

Luath Press Limited
committed to publishing well written books worth reading

LUATH PRESS takes its name from Robert Burns, whose little collie Luath (*Gael.*, swift or nimble) tripped up Jean Armour at a wedding and gave him the chance to speak to the woman who was to be his wife and the abiding love of his life. Burns called one of 'The Twa Dogs' Luath after Cuchullin's hunting dog in Ossian's *Fingal*. Luath Press was established in 1981 in the heart of Burns country, and now resides a few steps up the road from Burns' first lodgings on Edinburgh's Royal Mile.
Luath offers you distinctive writing with a hint of unexpected pleasures.

Most bookshops in the UK, the US, Canada, Australia, New Zealand and parts of Europe either carry our books in stock or can order them for you. To order direct from us, please send a £sterling cheque, postal order, international money order or your credit card details (number, address of cardholder and expiry date) to us at the address below. Please add post and packing as follows: UK – £1.00 per delivery address; overseas surface mail – £2.50 per delivery address; overseas airmail – £3.50 for the first book to each delivery address, plus £1.00 for each additional book by airmail to the same address. If your order is a gift, we will happily enclose your card or message at no extra charge.

Luath Press Limited
543/2 Castlehill
The Royal Mile
Edinburgh EH1 2ND
Scotland
Telephone: 0131 225 4326 (24 hours)
Fax: 0131 225 4324
email: sales@luath.co.uk
Website: www.luath.co.uk